PERGAMON CHESS SERIES

THE MACHINE PLAYS CHESS?

The Pergamon Chess Series

By The Same Author:

Games Playing with Computers 1972

First Computer Chess Conference (Ed.) 1973

The Turk

THE MACHINE PLAYS CHESS?

by

Alex G. Bell

PERGAMON PRESS

OXFORD · NEW YORK · TORONTO · SYDNEY · PARIS · FRANKFURT

U.K.	Pergamon Press Ltd., Headington Hill Hall, Oxford OX3 0BW, England
U.S.A.	Pergamon Press Inc., Maxwell House, Fairview Park, Elmsford, New York 10523, U.S.A.
CANADA	Pergamon of Canada Ltd., 75 The East Mall, Toronto, Ontario, Canada
AUSTRALIA	Pergamon Press (Aust.) Pty. Ltd., 19a Boundary Street, Rushcutters Bay, N.S.W. 2011, Australia
FRANCE	Pergamon Press SARL, 24 rue des Ecoles, 75240 Paris, Cedex 05, France
FEDERAL REPUBLIC OF GERMANY	Pergamon Press GmbH, 6242 Kronberg-Taunus, Pferdstrasse 1, Federal Republic of Germany

First edition 1978

Library of Congress Cataloging in Publication Data

Bell, A. G.
The machine plays chess?
(Pergamon chess series)

Bibliography: p.
1. Chess—Data processing. 2. Chess—Computer programs. I. Title.
GV1447.B44   1977   794.1'7   77–24302
ISBN 0–08–021221–2 Hard cover
ISBN 0–08–021222–0 Flexi cover

Printed in Great Britain by
Cox & Wyman Ltd
London, Fakenham and Reading

FOR MAGGIE

L'ordinateur rien
   remplacera la femme

Chess—is a foolish expedient for making idle people believe they are doing something very clever, when they are only wasting their time.

George Bernard Shaw

I do not think therefore I am not.

Dr. Strabismus of Utrecht

This interest in chess programs is a serious defect in your character.

Anon

Contents

Preface

THE machine plays chess—or does it? Is it, for example, a genuine machine and not an elaborate fraud? If it is a genuine machine, does it play chess like a human player? And if it is really an unbeatable chess machine, what else might it be able to do?

For well over a century chess machines have been built and the debate has raged over whether or not they are really playing chess. This book is a history of the debate and of some of the people who have been involved, including such great computer pioneers as Charles Babbage, John von Neumann, Alan Turing, Claud Shannon and Konrad Zuse. All of these people were fundamentally searching for unemotional intelligence—intelligence free from passion or self-interest. The irony is that they had to be so extremely passionate in their attempts to construct a dispassionate machine. Had they not been so, I doubt that I would have found the subject so interesting, and this book would not have been written.

At this point I should warn readers that they will not find out in these pages how to write a chess program, nor how to play chess. This is a book about people who have a passion for unemotional intelligence, written by someone who is by no means an unbiased observer. I hope that in writing it I have preserved something of the passion—and of the humour—that has been present during the evolution of the subject.

Those parts of the book where I have struck a more serious note reflect my belief that writing chess programs is a field of very pure research which not only reveals the strengths and weaknesses of general-purpose electronic computers, but can also tell us a great deal about ourselves and the way our brains work.

Whether this knowledge is of value or not is not for me to say. What I do know and can say is that a computer can match the ability of a human chess player in chess with only about 10 per cent of the 'over the board' experience—and it does this using techniques which only remotely resemble the way a human chooses a move. As Bobby Fischer had about 10,000 hours 'over the board' experience I find it pointless to speculate on the date a machine will reach his level. All that is required to settle the question is 1000 hours of big machine time, and at this moment this will not be easily obtained. A big computer costs about £1000 ($1800) per hour, so it would cost about £1,000,000 ($1,800,000).

So at the present time writing chess programs is just a hobby of mine—as also was writing this book. I would like to thank the many people who have helped me to indulge and thoroughly enjoy this serious defect in my character. In particular Dr. Jack Howlett who gave 30 hours of machine time to develop MASTER, a program which is currently the best in Western Europe, and also backed the organisation of two Computer Chess Conferences. Other people who helped me research this book include Lord Bowden, Alick Glennie, Dietrich Prinz, Donald Michie, Don Miguel Toros y Gallino, Fernando Garrido, Christopher Strachey, Jack Good, R. V. Jones, Mikhail Donskoy, Hans Berliner, Ron Atkin, John Scott, Richard Cichelli, Alan Bond, Nils Barricelli, Martin Gardner, Norton Jacobi, Thomas Caswell, David Slate and Larry Atkin. For typing the manuscript my thanks to Jean Jones and Margaret Arkwright. And last but not least, thanks to my old team who designed and wrote MASTER—John Birmingham and Peter Kent plus John Waldron, who taught MASTER how to play, and Chris Osland, who often ran it and missed the booze.

1976

A. G. BELL

CHAPTER 1

The Turk

IN 1769 the most famous chess-playing automaton of all time was built by
a 35-year-old engineering genius, Wolfgang von Kempelen, for the amuse-
ment of the Vienna Imperial Court. The automaton was a life-size figure
(see frontispiece), dressed in Turkish costume, seated behind a chest about
4ft (1·2 m) long, 2 ft (0·6 m) wide and 3 ft (0·9 m) high on which was placed
a chess board. The figure played chess with all-comers, moving the pieces
with its left hand. Before describing the machine's behaviour in greater
detail it is important to realise that very few people, then or now, seriously
believed the machine to be genuine. The moves it made were the product
of a human player and the fascination lay in trying to guess where the
human was hidden; how he followed the game; how he made the automaton move the pieces with its left hand and how (and this is most important), given all these handicaps, the player still managed to win most of the
games.

Kempelen's original intention was to demonstrate a 'telechiric' (Gr.
'distant hand') device, nowadays known as a waldo. The trick of hiding
the human manipulator was merely to add spice to a genuine piece of very
good engineering. Kempelen failed to appreciate that people have a fundamental desire to be fooled and amazed—witness nowadays the pheno-
menon of Uri Geller.

To Kempelen's consternation his conjuring trick was to become world
famous and his many, far more substantial achievements in hydraulics,
acoustics and magnetism were doomed to relative obscurity. The art of
conjuring, then and now, rarely depends on 'the quickness of the hand
deceiving the eye'. Terms such as legerdemain, prestidigitation, etc., are
incorrect; they imply rapidity of movement and absence of equipment.
Most conjurers depend on apparatus, natural physical phenomena and,
most important, the focusing of the attention of the audience on some

1

activity so that other movements will be disregarded—the classic 'misdirection of attention'.

Kempelen's automaton was to evolve through many levels of misdirection in its long career. Even now precisely how it was done at every stage of its career is not known but there is a wealth of detail to be found in contemporary descriptions by people who saw the machine in action. The Turk (as the machine was popularly known) was publicly exhibited between 1783 and 1838, a period of 55 years. Although the descriptions over this length of time naturally differ in detail, nevertheless the essentials remain the same, a tribute to Kempelen that no one could significantly improve his design.

When first shown to King Joseph II and the Vienna Imperial Court, Kempelen successfully gave the impression that the Turk was voice actuated! This was plausible because Kempelen had already built and demonstrated a machine that could talk. The machine had bellows, reeds and acoustic resonators, the 'control signals' were provided manually by moving a series of levers and it was reputed to have a remarkable performance, being capable of articulating about 30 words—an impressive demonstration of Kempelen's practical abilities and also his acoustical theories; theories of which he was proud and which he described in a book *The Mechanism of Human Speech*.* So it is hardly surprising that people believed the Turk to be voice actuated, of course it was—but what a pity it couldn't play chess of its own accord.

The problem of hiding a human in the machine was already solved. All Kempelen needed was a good chess player to guide it. However, chess players are not necessarily midgets and, as will become apparent, a double-double bluff was almost certainly the final result.

Whilst on tour in the 1780s a typical performance by the machine was as follows. In 1784 the Turk was exhibited in London, at 8 Savile Row, Burlington Gardens. The audience paid five shillings each for admission—equivalent to paying about £10 nowadays. Some of the best players in London had come to see and compete with the Turk but first the audience were allowed to see 'how' the Turk worked. The automaton was wheeled on to a stage and the many doors in the chest were all opened and shut whilst a candle was passed behind the chest. Finally the drawer at the bottom was pulled out, the chess pieces were taken out and set up for the first game. As the evening progressed and the Turk, to the accompaniment

* A book that was studied avidly by my namesake Alexander Graham Bell.

of great grinding and crunching, had beaten a number of people, more and more doors were left open. Finally even the drawer at the bottom was left open. At the end of the performance it became very difficult to imagine how a human could be hidden inside the machine—nevertheless one small compartment or another was always closed so the audience left marvelling at how the operator inside had shifted his position with such agility and still managed to beat good chess players on a board which must be out of his sight.

After Kempelen's death in 1804 the Turk was sold to a Bavarian musician, Johann Maelzel, who also had considerable mechanical ability but excelled Kempelen in showmanship. The most famous performance given by the machine under Maelzel was when it played Napoleon at Schonbrunn Castle, Vienna, in 1809. A popular story of this meeting concerned Napoleon's tendency to make illegal moves. Deliberately testing the powers of the automaton he made a false move. The automaton shook its head (it could do this), replaced the piece and motioned to Napoleon to move again. Highly amused, Napoleon played on—then made another false move. This time the machine removed the piece from the board and made its own move. Napoleon laughed and made another false move. The automaton raised its arm, swept all the pieces on to the floor and refused to continue.

This story is almost certainly pure fantasy—nobody would have dared to treat Napoleon in such a fashion. There is another version of this encounter which was circulated by Maelzel; this also is partly fabrication but is almost certainly nearer to the truth.

According to Maelzel the pieces *were* swept to the floor—but by Napoleon. From the start Napoleon refused to comply with the rules Maelzel had introduced. Unlike Kempelen, Maelzel insisted that the automaton's opponent should play on a separate board, both the opponent and the audience being outside a rope barrier. This was showmanship but Napoleon would have none of it—"We fight face to face!" and so he did, losing the game badly. According to Maelzel, Napoleon returned later with a magnet which he placed on the chess board, someone had apparently told him that the automaton depended on magnets for its operation. Maelzel says that he removed the magnet and the machine then won again easily. In the third and last game Napoleon wrapped a shawl round the face and body of the Turk. Like many other people he thought the operator was hidden inside the Turk's body with his arm inside the Turk's arm and following the game through a spy-hole. Again the machine won easily and, at this point, Napoleon brushed the pieces from the board and walked out.

There is no doubt that Napoleon did play the automaton on three occasions and lost all the games. He had, in fact, been playing the Austrian chess master Allgaier, one of the great players of his time, who was also in a situation where he was not afraid to beat the Emperor. Napoleon had only a vague idea of his own chess ability due to the number of sensible hypocrites and sycophants who lost to him on purpose in order not to incur his displeasure. The greatest complaint by some of these flatterers was that Napoleon was such a weak player that it was sometimes extremely difficult to lose without arousing his suspicions—the art of hustling was then in its infancy. What such performances certainly proved was that an ability to play good chess has little, if any, relation to the decision-making processes of generals and politicians.

Prince Eugene de Beauharnais, Napoleon's stepson via Josephine, was so intrigued after seeing this particular performance of the Turk that he offered Maelzel the equivalent of £25,000 if he would sell the automaton and reveal its secret. The deal was made and the Turk was taken to Italy where (typical of Napoleon's nepotism) Beauharnais was the viceroy.

The Turk languished in Milan until 1817. Beauharnais had lost interest when he discovered how it worked and he also had other, more pressing problems in the intervening years; notably a trip to Moscow and back in 1812 with his stepfather. Maelzel made a hire-purchase deal with Beauharnais in 1817 and took the machine on tour again. The players Maelzel employed in the next few years were many and varied, but always the best money could buy. They included Lewis, Williams and Mouret—wherever the Turk appeared it seemed that the local chess master would disappear. Unfortunately, although the automaton was as successful as ever, Maelzel got behind with his payments and, threatened with a legal suit, left Europe in 1826 for the New World.

Once again the Turk made headlines wherever it appeared. In America Maelzel employed a regular player, a young Frenchman named William Schlumberger, to decide the moves and no American player could defeat him. Schlumberger played for Maelzel for about 10 years and some of the best descriptions of the automaton in action come from this period. Probably the best known (and most inaccurate) analysis was the one by Edgar Allen Poe who saw an exhibition of the Turk in 1836. Poe published his theory of how the machine worked but seems to have been unaware of previous theories and experiments—in particular the alleged magnet and shawl experiments of Napoleon. Poe believed that Schlumberger was hidden inside the body of the Turk, viewing the board through a small hole. The analysis was incorrect in almost every detail except the identity of the player:

> There is a man, Schlumberger, who attends Maelzel wherever he goes but who has no ostensible occupation. This man is about medium size with a remarkable stoop to his shoulders. Whether he professes to play chess or not we are not informed. It is quite certain, however, that he is never to be seen during the exhibition of the Chess-Player, although frequently visible just before and just after the exhibition.

The other reasons Poe gave for his belief that a human was operating the machine are amusingly fallacious. Poe assumes, for example, that to build an unbeatable machine is not much more difficult than building a machine which wins most of its games. Therefore, as the automaton was not invincible, it must be operated by a human!

More practical arguments were made by an American reporter who noted that when someone in the audience shouted 'FIRE!' the cabinet began to shake as though someone was trying to get out.

Even more convincing proof came with the tragic end of the Turk's playing career. Schlumberger died of yellow fever in 1837 on a visit to Havana. The automaton was bought by a Mr. Ohe of Philadelphia who sold it, in 1840, to Dr. J. K. Mitchell, who reassembled the machine as a curiosity to be exhibited in the Chinese Museum at Philadelphia. It performed for a few weeks, but, without Maelzel's showmanship and Schlumberger's skill, it drew only small audiences. The illustration of the automaton was drawn at this time when the Turk, retired behind a glass enclosure, gazed lifelessly over his chess board at the occasional curious visitor. Fourteen years later, at the age of 85, it was destroyed in a fire on 8 July, 1854.

Two other automata were built in later years. 'Ajeeb' was dressed as an Egyptian and again cashed in on the popularity of a machine apparently beating a human in an intellectual activity—hardly surprising that it won many of its games as it was guided, for a while, by the chess master Pillsbury. In Europe Ajeeb was possibly even more successful than the Turk had been; over 100,000 people saw the machine in the span of 3 months when exhibited in Berlin in the 1870s—yet people nowadays still ask me what use is a machine that can play chess? (100,000 × £10 = £1,000,000 in 3 months.) Another automaton 'Mephisto' (guided by the chess master Gunsberg) actually won the first prize in an open tournament in 1878 after George McDonnel, the favourite, had withdrawn because the automaton's identity was not revealed.

Alas none of these machines still exists. Ajeeb suffered the same fate as the Turk, lost in a fire in 1929 in America. And Mephisto? After a relatively short career of about 10 years it was broken up in England around about 1880.

So how did these automata work? There still exists a wealth of evidence, observation, theory and wild guesses. Much of this material is conflicting and some of it deliberately misleading. People saw what they wanted to see whilst Maelzel and others misdirected their attention—but some details are consistent. Maelzel always allowed American audiences a supervised inspection of the Turk and his chest before a performance. As with Kempelen, various doors and compartments were opened and closed in order to convince people that the player must be hidden in the bottom drawer. At the start of play the audience would have to withdraw behind a barrier— the drawer was opened and the chess pieces taken out. The player must have moved into the body of the Turk. But how could he see the board? Unlike blindfold exhibitions these games were often played in silence. Underneath the chess board were 64 small magnetic discs, each on a thread. The chess pieces were made of iron, so—obviously—the game could be, indeed must be, followed by observing the rise and fall of these discs. Oddly enough Poe seems unaware of these discs although Maelzel would have us believe that Napoleon suspected their presence and purpose. The movement of the arm and the grasping of the conical chess pieces was a genuine piece of pantographic engineering, parts of which can be seen in the illustration. Magnets were used to help the fingers hold the pieces.

So the best analysis, indeed the one which has been believed for the last 100 years, is that Schlumberger (amongst other deformed chess masters) was partly in the Turk's legs, partly behind the false back of the drawer, that he was following the game by watching discs move up and down and finally, that the Turk's arm was moved by a telechiric device of levers and straps, requiring some expertise to operate into which Schlumberger had inserted his own arm. The problem with this, the accepted analysis, is the number of people who played for Maelzel in the period of 1818 to 1820. At least six chess masters were employed in this period—all of various shapes and sizes, all of whom apparently had to learn to follow a game from the movement of discs, all of whom had to learn how to move the pieces remotely and, most important, all of whom had to win as many games as possible—the success at the box office depended on winning games far more than any other feature of the performance.

It seems to me extremely unlikely that it was necessary or desirable for the chess master to actually be inside the machine himself. It is far more likely that the operator was a trained boy (or very small adult) who followed the directions of the chess player who was hidden elsewhere on the stage or in the theatre—the Turk was a 'mind-reading' act. Nowadays the techniques of passing information non-verbally are better known. The simplest code for the Turk's operator would be a set of signals for start, left, right, up, down and stop. These signals can be made in a variety of ways (hand in pocket, stance, head movements, etc.) particularly on a stage with audience kept back. It is certainly difficult to believe that any human who must perform efficiently (and therefore as comfortably as possible) would subject himself to the confines of the Turk's chest particularly if a boy could hide himself more easily within the machine. Unfortunately we shall never know.

CHAPTER 2

Torres y Quevedo

BORN in 1852 in Santa Cruz, Spain, Leonardo Torres y Quevedo is considered by many people familiar with his work to have been the equal of Thomas Edison in the field of invention.

Torres' speciality was electromechanical devices; the next step forward in telechiric mechanisms after the levers and pulleys used by the so-called frauds of the Turk and other chess-playing automata. In his long career he designed and built a number of remotely controlled devices including a guidance system which successfully steered a boat through Bilbao harbour.

Probably his most significant development was the guided torpedo. The problems of keeping a torpedo at a constant depth and on a constant heading are not usually appreciated by the layman who apparently thinks (in both senses) that torpedos, like bullets, maintain a straight course by sheer inertia.

In building a device to maintain a torpedo at constant depth (a pressure sensor linked to a horizontal rudder) Torres was struck by the 'intelligence' of the mechanism. Admittedly the problem was restricted and specialised but his device could 'solve' the problem far more quickly and accurately than any human.

In order to demonstrate more clearly that many other 'intelligent' activities can, if analysed, be reproduced by simple mechanical devices, Torres designed and built a machine to play the simple chess end game of White King and Rook vs. Black King.

I first became interested in the literature of chess programs in 1962 and, during the intervening years, I came across many references to Torres' chess machine which were downright contradictory; in particular Bowden (see Chapter 3) says the machine was made 'in about 1890', whereas Shannon gives 'in 1914'; a difference of 24 years and neither author describes how the machine worked. I was therefore pleased to accept an

8

invitation from Señor Don Miguel Toros y Gallino to visit Spain in June 1974 and see Torres' machine in action for myself.

The machine is now in the Escuela Tecnica Superior de Ingenieros de Caminos (The School of Road Works) of the Polytechnic University, Madrid. Almost the first thing one notices is that it has a loudspeaker (see photograph) with which it can pronounce 'check' and 'mate' from a gramophone record; the principle is similar to the speaking clock on the telephone.

The machine is beautifully preserved and still works. The human player has the Black king and this piece is moved by sliding it diagonally from the centre of its square into channels between the squares, along the rank or file channel and then diagonally into the new square. The piece is mechanically linked beneath the board and the machine can therefore follow the move and, if illegal, will object twice verbally and on the third occasion refuse to continue playing.

In programming terms such sophistication is usually called 'the icing on the cake'. I was more curious to know when the machine was built and, assuming legal play, precisely how it calculated its moves.

Torres apparently built a prototype machine about 1890 which went through a number of sporadic refinements. His final version made its most publicised performance at the Paris World Fair in 1914 but it, understandably, sank into oblivion on the outbreak of World War I. So much for the discrepancy in dates.

As Sherlock Holmes observed to Dr. Watson in *The Case of the Dancing Men*, most clever things are simple when explained. Torres' machine is no exception. To begin with the machine was not 'efficient', it always checkmated in the lower most row (see Fig. 1) and could take more than 50 moves to do this; technically the game is then drawn.

The 'algorithm' of the machine is as follows, the board is divided into three parts: two 'rook zones' either side of the two central files (Fig. 1).

The machine asks the following questions in order and, if true, takes the corresponding action. It then waits for the opponents' next move.

(1) If the Black king is in the same zone as the rook then move rook to opposite side of board (the move in the diagram), else

(2) if vertical distance between Black king and rook greater than one, then rook down one square, else

(3) if vertical distance between kings greater than two then White king down one square, else

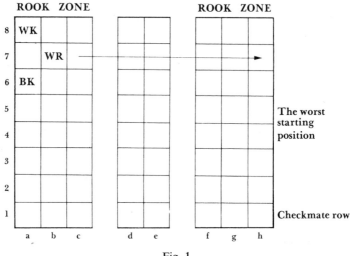

Fig. 1

(4) if horizontal distance between kings is odd then rook one square horizontally, else

(5) if horizontal distance between kings is zero then rook down one square, else

(6) king one square horizontally towards Black king.

One of these questions must get a true answer (unless the last move by the opponent was illegal), so the machine is never lost for a response. Also these simple questions and responses show a fair degree of chess knowledge: (1) Defence; (2) and (3) Approach; (4) Tempo; (5) Check and checkmate; and (6) Opposition. Nevertheless the strategy (now revealed) is seen to be simple and plodding. For example, a human opponent who is aware of the 'style' of the machine can, from the starting position in the diagram, force the machine to take 61 moves to effect the mate.

The machine has other deficiencies; it always started with its king and rook in a8 and b7 (as shown) and allowed the opponent to choose only the initial square of the Black king. If the opponent chose a square in the top row (c, d, e, f, g or h8) then the demonstrator had to transpose the Black king into the 'equivalent' square in the (a) file or the algorithm could not work.

Torres' daughter removed some of these deficiencies and demonstrated a much-improved version of her father's machine at the Brussel's World Fair in 1958 but (as far as I could ascertain in my schoolboy Spanish) the machine I saw was Torres' original 1914 model.

Unfortunately no literature appears to exist on the precise alterations. The probable reason for this is that by 1958 Torres' machine had been superseded by the performance of general-purpose electronic computers and is now a genuine museum piece which, unlike the Turk, has been fortunately preserved.

CHAPTER 3

The Paper Machines

ABOUT 1840, Charles Babbage, an English mathematician, had completed the design of his 'Analytical Engine'. This machine, although never built, foreshadowed many of the features of the modern electronic computer, but its fate does not concern us at the moment.

With most of the drawings and details of the Engine finished, Babbage— a rather conceited, arrogant man—

> began to meditate upon the intellectual means by which I had reached to such advanced and even to such unexpected results . . . I felt, however, that it would be more satisfactory to the minds of others, and even in some measure to my own, that I should try the power of such principles as I had laid down, by assuming some question of an entirely new kind, and endeavouring to solve it by the aid of those principles which had so successfully guided me in other cases.
>
> After much consideration I selected for my test the contrivance of a machine that should be able to play a game of purely intellectual skill successfully; such as . . . chess.

Babbage goes on to relate how he discussed this idea with other people: "I endeavoured to ascertain the opinions of persons in every class of life and of all ages, whether they thought it required human reason to play games of skill. The almost constant answer was in the affirmative."

But Babbage did not agree with this opinion, he believed that "every game of skill is susceptible of being played by an automaton" and his proof was roughly this:

The automaton is given a position in the game and it then asks the following questions:

(1) Is the position legal? If not, complain.

(2) Have I lost? If so, resign.

(3) Have I won? If so, claim it.

(4) Can I win in the next move? If so, make it.

(5) Is opponent about to win? If so, prevent him.

(6) If neither of us can win at the next move I must look for a move which gives me two different ways of winning, my opponent can only block one way so I will produce situation (4) above.

If all these cases fail the automaton must look ahead to three or more successive moves.

Now it would be nice to record that Babbage was the inventor of the mini-max principle; the searching ahead through a tree of possibilities which most modern chess programs use. Unfortunately his proof has logical flaws in it and is not very rigorous, these errors are mainly due to him only considering noughts and crosses as the game in question.

Actually Babbage appears to have seen little difference between noughts and crosses and the much more complicated game of chess: "Allowing one hundred moves on each side for the longest game at chess, I found that the combinations involved in the Analytical Engine enormously surpassed any required, even by the game of chess." At this point he was definitely talking through his Victorian hat.

Another example of how Babbage only groped with the right questions is the problem he raises of what to do when the automaton had two ways of winning a game: "In this case no reason existed within the machine to direct its choice: unless some provision were made the machine would attempt two contradictory motions." The situation would be disastrous as a donkey starving to death between two equidistant bales of hay. However, the old adage 'First come, first served' naturally resolves this ambiguity in the sequential machine and it is surprising that Babbage could not see this simple answer.

Babbage never built his game-playing automaton because, as he put it, "it would occupy too much of my own time to contrive and execute the machinery".

After this first, fumbling attempt to mechanise the full game of chess almost 100 years were to pass before the question was again discussed, but this time the questioners were men of greater ability and accomplishment with the added advantage of access to machinery and technology that Babbage would have envied and yet, oddly enough, probably have understood.

In 1939 the British Foreign Office established its Department of Communications at Bletchley, a town in Buckinghamshire about 50 miles north of London. The main purpose of this innocently named department was to intercept and decode the enemy's radio signals; in particular the German

ENIGMA machine cipher. Some of the best mathematicians, linguists and electronic engineers in Britain were gathered together, plus the two best chess players in the country at the time, Harry Golombek and C. H. O'D. Alexander.

Their inclusion at the time was not entirely due to any chess ability. Nevertheless Professor R. V. Jones, the man who almost single handedly unravelled the German radar defence system, later wrote: "As regards the connection between chess playing and decipherment, this was very conspicuous to some of us during the War."

In order to unravel the German defences Jones had much help from Bletchley, but how the German codes were deciphered is not the subject of this book and even if it were, the place and time is still too shrouded in mystery; the technical documentation of the machines built at Bletchley is, nearly 35 years later, still classified.

What is known is that these machines, in particular the Collissi series, were forerunners of the modern electronic computer. Unlike the general-purpose computer the Collissi were specialised in solving the statistical problems of decipherment, this they did with enormous speed and great success under the special security classification, TOP SECRET ULTRA.* Churchill himself so valued this source of information that he considered it preferable to lose a battle than to compromise this vital source of Intelligence.

Probably the most prominent mathematician at Bletchley was Alan Mathieson Turing, then in his early thirties. Amongst Turing's many interests was a fascination for automata and the game of chess; I. J. Good, his main statistical assistant, later recalled "Some of our discussions were concerned with the possibilities of machine intelligence, and especially with automatic chess-playing. We agreed that the most interesting aspect of this topic would be the extent to which the machine might be able to simulate human thought processes. Of course we did not overlook the notion of a true search, with truncation and evaluation at quiescent positions. This procedure seemed obvious to us long before Shannon's paper was published, and I made the mistake of thinking it was not worth publishing. We did not think of the alpha–beta algorithm, which was suggested by John McCarthy much later and is *not* obvious."

And so there seems little doubt that the man-versus-machine chess-

---

* Collissi were still being used as late as 1957.

playing argument really began at Bletchley with Turing playing a major role. One possible reason for his interest is that, despite his brilliance and depth of thought, he was an absolute duffer at the game. Harry Golombek later commented on the irrelevancy of IQ to chess ability: "Conversely, I have also known some of the world's finest brains and some of these, though passionately fond of chess, have been pretty poor players. I used to know one of the world's leading mathematicians and whenever we played chess I had to give him the odds of a Queen in order to make matters more equal, and even then I always won."

It is difficult to estimate Turing's influence on the real work at Bletchley Park. His notebooks of the time are now in a vault somewhere in London and are still classified; some of the pages have, reputedly, drawings of chess positions with notes. Nevertheless his influence must have been significant as he was eventually awarded an OBE for his war work, a medal which he rather typically kept in a box of odds and ends.

At the end of the war Turing received a large grant from the British Government to build a general-purpose electronic computer at the National Physical Laboratory near London. This machine, unlike the specialised Collissi, would be capable of solving a variety of problems, particularly in the important new fields of atomic weapons research and ballistics. Turing had published the mathematical concept of such a machine as early as 1936 but turning his ideas into a reality was not an easy task. Although there had been enormous advances in electronic technology during the war—particularly the pulse techniques of radar—just how to use this new technology to build a general-purpose computer was not at all clear. For example, the new machine would have to have an electronic 'memory' and the only candidates for this purpose at the time were the mercury delay line and the cathode-ray tube; both devices having been developed to overcome jamming of night-fighter radar systems (they did this by 'remembering' and removing stationary objects, e.g. the surrounding terrain and 'window',* and therefore displayed only moving objects—the possible target aircraft). In 1946 Turing did not believe that either of these devices could be used as a permanent memory to store information because the memory was transient, only lasting some few thousandths of a second.

In this practical respect Turing was wrong but his contributions to the newly developing theoretical subject of Numerical Analysis are well recorded and show that he had a firm grasp of how computers (built by

* Strips of tinfoil which gave similar echoes to a large aircraft.

other people) could be instructed to solve a variety of mathematical problems.

Turing's interest in Machine Intelligence, and mechanised chess in particular, was also maintained. A newspaper report in 1946 has this to say about his proposed machine, the Automatic Computing Engine (ACE). "The machine is to be an improvement on the American ENIAC, and it was in the brain of Dr. Turing that the more efficient model was developed. Dr. Turing, speaking about the 'memory' of the new brain, said . . . 'it will be able to retain for a week or more about as much as an actor can learn in an average play'." In the same interview Turing discussed, for the first time in public, the possibility of such machines being able to play an average game of chess—"that is a question we may be able to settle experimentally in about 100 years time".

Nowadays computers play better than average chess so Turing was rather pessimistic. But this belief is hardly surprising since many problems delayed the realisation of Turing's ambitious ACE design and eventually, in 1949, he resigned from the Government and accepted the appointment of Assistant Director of the Computing Laboratory at Manchester University.

The reason for this move was that the University had a working computer with a sizeable, fast C.R.T. memory—8 pages of 64 words of 20 bits.* Also, as no Director had been appointed, Turing could do whatever he liked with, what was then, one of the most powerful computers in the world.

In 1951, Dr. (now Lord) Bowden of Manchester University decided to write a popular book about the new 'Electronic Brains'. The public had become aware of these machines because of some astounding feats of moronic arithmetic, for example, calculating π to 2000 places, and Bowden's book *Faster than Thought* was one of the first attempts to explain the new technology to the layman. The book is still well worth reading because a quarter of a century ago there were probably only about twenty practising full-time programmers in England and all of them were either at or visiting Manchester. Bowden asked all of them to contribute to his book and Turing, a pioneer in almost all aspects of computing, surprisingly elected to write about Digital Computers applied to Games, in particular the game of chess.

Ever since his Bletchley days Turing had been developing a 'paper' chess

* This machine was built on a Collissi chassis. See Chapter 4 for more details.

machine. This machine was a set of rules from which one could calculate, in the order of a few minutes, an unambiguous move for any legal position. Developed in collaboration with an old Bletchley colleague, David Champernowne, Turing had made one attempt to play this set of rules against another paper machine designed by Donald Michie and Shawn Wylie (also old Bletchley colleagues), but the game had proved too tedious to complete.

In early 1952 Turing had a rough draft of his paper for Bowden's book and, like Babbage, he decided to put his ideas to the test—the resulting game is the first recorded chess game between man and machine.

Turing only mentions the opponent as "a weak player who did not know the system". This nameless opponent was Alick Glennie, then 26 years old, a graduate of Edinburgh University who was at Manchester in order to learn the technology and techniques of electronic computation for his secret work on the British atomic weapons project. Glennie was (and still is) a highly talented programmer who later designed the first compiler; however, he still admits to being a weak chess player.

Bowden in his book implies that this historic game took place before November 1951 but Glennie, who arrived in July 1951, believes it was sometime in 1952. The location he remembers clearly; Turing's office on the first floor of the Royal Society Computing Laboratory which was at the side of the Schuster Physics Building (where Rutherford first split the atom).

As I remember, he persuaded me over lunch to take part in his chess experiment. I just happened to be there and was willing to take part on the spur of the moment. It was played in the afternoon, in his office, a rather bare place with a small table untidy with paper. We had a chess board with pieces and Turing had his select rules written on about six sheets of paper somewhat mixed up with other paper.

Laboratory gossip had told me that mechanical chess was one of Turing's interests so there were very few preliminaries before we started to play. He did explain briefly what he wanted. You can see the recorded game. It seemed to go rather slowly and I think I got slightly bored as I was not a keen player and had not played much before or since—I knew a few standard openings but none of the finer points of strategy. I was indeed a weak player: chess was for me a pleasant relaxation for odd moments with other weak players.

During the game Turing was working to his rules and was clearly having difficulty playing to them because they often picked moves which he knew were not the best. He also made a few mistakes in following his rules which had to be backtracked. This would occur when he was pondering the validity of White's last move while I was considering my move. There may have been other mistakes in following his rules that escaped notice—possibly they could be detected from the record of the game. He had a tendency to think he knew the move the rules would produce and then have second thoughts. He would then try to find the piece of paper containing that section of the rules, and to do so would start juggling with all his papers. We were playing on a small table which did not help.

The game took 2 or 3 hours. Turing's reaction to the progress of the play was mixed; exasperation at having to keep to his rules; difficulty in actually doing so; and interest in the experiment and the disasters into which White was falling. Of course, he could see them coming. I remember it as a rather jolly afternoon and I believe Turing must have enjoyed it too—in his way.

Glennie won the game at the 29th move. The position was (Fig. 2) and

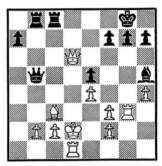

Fig. 2

R–Q1 wins the White queen so the program resigned 'on the advice of his trainer' (Turing's words).

How did Turing's program work? First Turing gave it the traditional 'evaluation of material' P=1, N=3, B=3½, R=5, Q=10, K=1000.

The program considered all White's moves and all Black's replies. If White could capture at this depth (i.e. one move ahead or, in computer chess jargon, two plies ahead) because of a forced sequence then the capture, recapture sequence was followed until a 'dead position' was reached, i.e. no more captures or mates in the next ply. The resulting 'dead positions' were evaluated on a material basis of W/B and the "most material winning or least material losing move" was made.

In many positions, particularly in the opening, the above rule is ambiguous, e.g. there is no distinction between the 'best' 12 of the 20 possible opening moves. Turing overcame this with a 'position play value' as follows:

All the White men *plus* the Black king have a position-play contribution for White.

(i) For the Q, R, B or N, count their mobility as (the square root of the number of legal moves it can make +1·0 if it can capture) + ((if not a Q) 1·0 if defended +0·5 if defended twice or more).

(ii) For the K, count mobility as above + (1·0 if castling is possible, 2·0 if castling is possible at the next move, 3·0 for actually castling) − (N.B. minus) vulnerability which is the mobility of a friendly queen on the same square as the king.

(iii) For the P's count +0·2 for each rank advanced +0·3 if defended by a piece (not a pawn).

(iv) For the BK count +0·5 for check, 1·0 for threat of checkmate.

Position play value is always calculated for resulting positions with similar material value. Finally, to simplify the calculations, the square-roots were rounded off and written on one of Turing's pieces of paper thus:

0	1	2	3	4	5	6	7	8	9	10
0	1	1·4	1·7	2	2·2	2·4	2·6	2·8	3	3·2

So now we can see how Turing's machine calculated its opening move. First, no pawns forward one square give any possibility of capture. Of the remaining 12 possibilities P–K4 is best because from (i) Q= +2, KB= +2·2, KN = +0·3 = 4·5; and from (ii) K = +1-1·4 = −0·4; and from (iii) KP = +0·4−0·3 (no longer defended by K) = 0·1; and the total is an increase in position play value of 4·2, an increase which is greater than that achieved by any of the other 11 'aggressive' opening moves.

To continue, the second move N–QB3 is calculated thus:

from (i)   QN = +0·8 (added mobility)
                    +0·5 (now defended twice)
              QR = +1·0 (mobility)
              QB = +0·5 (now defended twice)
and from (iii)   KP = +0·3 (defended by QN)

giving a total increase of 3·1 which is again greater than the position-play value of any other move.

The third move, P–Q4, is best because of the increased mobility (2·6) of the Q and QB. And so the game continues with white having little idea where or what anything is on the board; it is quite defenceless against a fork, for example.

To the interested reader it is an illuminating exercise to recalculate the

moves of Turing's paper machine. As an added incentive, note that one of
the moves chosen is in error—as Glennie said, Turing had a tendency to
think he knew the move.

Game between Turing's Machine and Alick Glennie

No random choices arose in this game. The increase in position-play value
is given when relevant, an * indicates that all other moves have a lower
value.

	TUROCHAMP		GLENNIE
1	P–K4	4·2*	P–K4
2	N–QB3	3·1*	N–KB3
3	P–Q4	2·6*	B–N5
4	N–B3	2·0	P–Q3
5	B–Q2	3·5*	N–B3
6	P–Q5	0·2	N–Q5
7	P–KR4	1·1*	B–N5
8	P–QR4	1·0*	N×N+
9	P×N		B–KR4
10	B–N5+	2·4*	P–B3
11	P×P		0–0
12	P×P		R–N1
13	B–QR6	−1·5	Q–R4
14	Q–K2	0·6	N–Q2
15	R–KN1	1·2*	N–B4
16	R–N5		B–N3
17	B–N5	0·4	N×NP
18	0–0–0	3·2*	N–B4
19	B–B6		KR–QB1
20	B–Q5		B×N
21	B×B	0·7	Q×P
22	K–Q2		N–K3
23	R–N4	0·3	N–Q5
24	Q–Q3		N–N4
25	B–N3		Q–R3
26	B–B4		B–R4

TUROCHAMP	GLENNIE
27 R–N3	Q–R5
28 B×N	Q×B
29 Q×P	R–Q1

Turing was fully aware of the weaknesses of his paper machine, he ruefully described it as a caricature of his own play, making oversights similar to his own because neither of them reliably chose the strong moves for analysis. Despite (or maybe because of?) this observation Turing believed it quite possible that a computer chess program could be written that would be able to beat him and, after the Glennie game, he did begin to program the university computer (variously called MADM, Ferranti Mk 1 or Manchester Mk 2) to play the game. But he was not a good programmer, his brilliant mind did not have the persistence or patience for the boring trivia required to make a big program work and also this was only a spare-time project. He died in mysterious circumstances on 8 June 1954. The man who had done so much to pioneer computing in Britain and had contributed enormously to the solving of ENIGMA, became an enigma of his own. In retrospect his death also marked the end of a British superiority in computer technology and software and America took her rightful place as the leader.

Claud Elwood Shannon was born in Michigan in 1916. One of the great American pioneers in the development and application of electronic computing, his career resembled that of Turing in many ways—both men had spent a year before the war at Princeton with John von Neumann (one of the world's greatest mathematicians who devised the Theory of Games and also developed the stored program concept; the fundamental principle of the general-purpose machine).

Both Turing and Shannon worked on automating crypto-analysis (code breaking) during the war and, possibly because of this, both were interested in machine intelligence in general and mechanised chess in particular—yet there is no record of them ever meeting or discussing these common interests and experiences.

In March 1949 Shannon gave a talk in which he described, for the first time and in much more explicit detail than Turing's later paper, how an electronic computer could be instructed to play chess using a mini–max procedure, i.e. by looking ahead about three moves and backing up the best line on the basis of a (necessarily) simple evaluation function. Some of his proposals are described later in Chapter 9. More interesting are the points made by Shannon which have been relatively overlooked so far.

Shannon defended the idea of a chess machine because "although of no practical importance, the question is of theoretical interest . . . chess is generally considered to require 'thinking' for skilful play; a solution of this problem will force us either to further restrict our concept of 'thinking' or to admit the possibility of mechanised thought".

Shannon did not define what is 'a solution of this problem' but modern chess programs are quite strong players and convincingly demonstrate mechanised thought.

Like Turing, Shannon gave an example of a simple evaluation function which can be applied at quiescent (or dead) positions. He took the relative values of K, Q, R, B, N and P as 200, 9, 5, 3, 3 and 1 respectively; he then penalised, doubled, backward and isolated (D, S, I) pawns as the loss of half a pawn and rewarded mobility (M) by adding one-tenth of a pawn for every legal move thus:

Evaluation of position $= 200(K–k) + 9(Q–q) + 5(R–r) + 3(BN–bn) + (P–p) + 0\cdot1(M–m) - 0\cdot5(D–d + S–s + I–i)$. *Note.* Small letters are opponent's pieces, etc.

Shannon believed that such a simple evaluation function applied to a tree search of 3 moves (or 6 plies) ahead would (a) take too long; at least 16 minutes and (b) still be a weak player. In these beliefs he was mistaken, tree searching does not have to be exhaustive because of the alpha–beta principle (again see Chapter 9) and also a program which searches 3 moves ahead can, with even the simple evaluation given by Shannon, often play surprisingly well—depth can overcome a vast amount of ignorance and 3 moves ahead, even nowadays, is a respectable depth.

Shannon made suggestions as to how forcing lines can be followed deeper than 3 moves (e.g. always follow a sequence of checks; always complete a sequence of capture, recapture down to the quiescent, dead position, etc.) and only now are some of his proposals being implemented in an efficient manner.

However, one proposal that has not, even now, been implemented efficiently is that the machine should be capable of learning from its mistakes, i.e. never be beaten in the same way twice. Many modern chess programs overcome this weakness by having a store of 'book openings' from which they select randomly their first 1 to (possibly) 10 moves before beginning to mini–max, i.e. generate, search, evaluate and back up.

Another proposal by Shannon was intended as an alternative to brute-force searching. However, this alternative strategy would require far, far more chess 'knowledge' than the simple "value of pieces + mobility — pawn defects" that he had already discussed and "would require a rather formidable analysis of the game. Although there are various books analysing combination play and the middle game, they are written for human consumption, not for computing machines. It is possible to give a person one or two specific examples of a general situation and have him understand and apply the general principles involved."

To give a computer this ability is, indeed, a 'formidable' task. Coming under the general heading of Machine or Artificial Intelligence this approach has not been very successful to date. Nevertheless Shannon believed that "if this were done, a much more efficient program would result".

One final quote: "It is not being suggested that we should design the strategy in our own image. Rather it should be matched to the capacities and weaknesses of the computer. The computer is strong in speed and accuracy and weak in analytical ability and recognition. Hence it should make more use of brutal calculations than humans." In retrospect Shannon was probably the first man to discuss the current controversy (and anti-pathy) between the two approaches of Brute Force (or Crunch) and the School of Knowledge.

Finally, an anecdote by Richard Sprague which includes Shannon and von Neumann. It is difficult to précis Sprague's story about the last of the paper machines without losing much of its humour and how it also under-lines the perpetual interest of the press and the public in the subject, an interest which has continued from The Turk to the present day.

THE CHESS PLAYING CRC 102
BY RICHARD SPRAGUE*

At the time of the unveiling of the 102 in Hawthorne in 1951, the management had obtained an OK from the Air Force for a publicity release on the machine before shipping it to the Cambridge Air Force Research Laboratories in Massachusetts. As Vice-President of Marketing I arranged for a press conference and demonstration at CRC, and several local members of the press attended. One was a reporter from the *Hawthorne Daily News*. He asked me, "Just what is this device, anyway? What will it do?" After I had run through my prepared set of material, he said ,"No, I mean really

* From *Communication of the ACM*, July 1972.

what makes this machine different? Can it think?" I explained as best I could the analogy between human thought processes and logical operations in a programmed computer, but the reporter didn't understand, and finally I asked him if he would consider chess playing as a thinking process. When he said Yes, I replied that the power of the stored program idea was so great that eventually computers of this type would be able to play a decent game of chess. I emphasized that the programs would have to be written by experts and that machines would have to be a lot faster with much greater memory than the 102. Then he asked whether the computer would always win if it played against a chess expert. I said that would depend on the programs, speed and memory, and whether a learning program was built into the machine. I said under these conditions the computer might win often.

The next day, Friday, a few lines appeared in the Los Angeles papers using our press kit material, and a story appeared in the *Hawthorne Daily News* saying that the CRC 102, an electronic brain which can think, was demonstrated at CRC. The story misquoted me as saying that the 102 could play chess against a human being and would always win.

The other officers of CRC were quite upset over this, but I assured them that I would call the reporter on Monday and get it all straightened out. I reminded them that the *Hawthorne Daily News* circulation was rather limited. I didn't know that United Press had somehow picked up the Hawthorne paper's story and would release it all over the United States on Saturday.

I was awakened on Sunday morning by a telephone call from United Press in New York wanting to know what CRC was going to do about the chess challenge out of Washington, D.C. When I sleepily asked what chess challenge he was talking about, he said, "You mean you haven't heard about some fellow named Jacobs challenging your computer to a chess match?"

The name Jacobs woke me up fast. One of our few competitors in 1951 (IBM had not begun, and Eckert & Mauchly were not competing with the 102) was the Jacobs Instrument Company in Bethesda, Maryland. Don Jacobs' small general-purpose machine had us only a little worried. The reporter told me about the Hawthorne paper's story appearing in the *Washington Post* and Jacob's offering to bet $1000 that he could beat the CRC in a chess match. Jacobs' strategy seemed obvious to me: gain attention and then announce *his* general purpose computer.

The U.P. man asked me what we were going to do about the challenge and I said I would call him back. Then I tried to reach one of my colleagues for consultation, but they were all away for the weekend. I finally got hold of Harold Sarkissian and asked what we should do. Harold said, "You're the Vice-President of marketing. You figure it out." So, I called the U.P. man back and made the following remarks. First, we would not be able to accept Mr Jacobs' challenge on his terms. The computer would obviously have to be fed each move made by Jacobs. Secondly, I said that it would take time to program the computer to play chess and that we would need the assistance of someone who had already been writing chess playing programs. I mentioned Claud Shannon of Bell Labs and John von Neumann of Princeton.* I said that CRC would accept the challenge on the condition that either of those two men was allowed to help write the programs. Third, I placed a condition on the match which would require Jacobs to inform the 102 in advance of the chess system he would use.

* *Author's note:* Turing, Shannon and von Neumann all wrote chess programs. Von Neumann actually gave a talk on the subject in San Diego in 1952, but no record of this is available.

I thought, in my *naïveté*, that these conditions would end the matter, figuring that either the press or Jacobs would drop it. I was wrong. The next day the U.P. printed two stories, the first misquoting me as saying, "Our boy will take him apart", and that we were eager to meet Jacobs' challenge as long as Claude Shannon or John von Neumann would *referee* the match and if Jacobs would let us know his chess system and agree to a time limit on the match. The second article quoted Jacobs as saying he would agree to a match under our terms, although he would not give his system to the computer because with that information anyone could beat him.

My telephone started ringing at 8.30 a.m. and didn't stop for days. United Press and Associated Press called for follow-up stories. The Mutual Newsreel of the Air (radio) asked to interview me. CBS radio said they would send a crew out to 'the brain factory' to do a taped broadcast. The producer of Edward R. Murrow's 'See It Now' program phoned to ask whether the 102 could be shipped to New York to appear on the TV show. *Life* magazine wanted to set up a chess match in a giant hall somewhere in Los Angeles with a cover story titled "Life Goes to a Chess Match". A local TV show wanted us to bring the 102 down to the Hollywood studio where the M.C. would play chess against the machine. (He had sword swallowers and wrestling bears on the same show.) The producer of the Dean Martin and Jerry Lewis show asked if we could bring the computer to the show so that Lewis could play chess with it. (Jerry would win of course.)

To our surprise the public relations office for the Air Force in Washington was delighted with the publicity. They had heard from the 'See It Now' producer and asked whether we could ship the machine to Washington for a press conference there before sending it to New York for the Murrow program.

To avoid the admission that the machine could never play chess, which would embarrass the Air Force, we decided to explain that while the computer would be able to play Mr Jacobs, given enough time to get ready, it was scheduled for far more important defense work at Cambridge Air Force Research Laboratories. Thereby we graciously ducked the matter.

Today computer chess matches are commonplace; the exaggerations of the 1950s fade a little. Still, the dream of the 102 and Jacobs placed head-to-head in the center of the cavernous Elks Hall in Los Angeles, the TV cameras trained on them, John von Neumann there as referee, and *Life* magazine reporters and cameras covering the event, has a certain appeal to it.

CHAPTER 4

The First Programs

THE first chess 'program' was that of Torres y Quevedo which has already been discussed. Although it is quite feasible (and more 'efficient') to build specialised machines to play chess and only chess, this would be extremely expensive. Most chess programs run on general-purpose computers and the very first one was written by Dr. Dietrich Gunther Prinz at Manchester University in 1951.

Prinz had heard rumours about the Sprague challenge: "In a report to the *Manchester Guardian* (13 November 1951) Alistair Cooke mentioned an American firm which was said to have challenged any human chess player to a match against its electronic machine. However, inquiries in the United States failed to confirm this report and it seems that *the first concrete approach* to the problem is my work carried out on the machine installed at the University of Manchester."

Before discussing what Prinz did let us take a closer look at this machine which played such a prominent part in the early days of games-playing programs.

The first Manchester University computer was a small experimental machine that Professor F. C. Williams had built in 1948 to test his storage tube memory—however, "The machine that I used for the chess program was the one built by Ferranti for the University. There is some confusion about names. The University wanted to call them Mark I and Mark II; for some time the Ferranti machine was known as Madam (at one occasion it was called 'Joe' by the *Daily Express*); finally it was called Ferranti Mk I. The next machine, Mk II, became the Mercury"—followed by ATLAS, MU4 and currently (1975) the University is developing MU5. However, back to MADM (the machine's correct name) and Prinz.

"The electronic store of this machine consisted of eight cathode ray tubes or 'pages'. Each page had 64 half words of 20 bits each. The magnetic

26

backing store consisted of two drums or 'wheels'. Each wheel had 256 'tracks' and each track corresponded to two pages. Transfers could be made between a half-track and a page (tube), or a full track and two consecutive pages, at a time.''

So we have this picture of the machine's memory (Fig. 3).

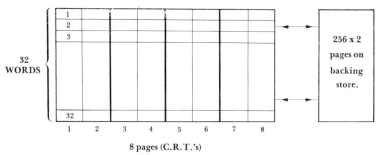

8 pages (C.R.T.'s)

Fig. 3

Transfers from tube to track were called 'up transfers', from track to tube 'down transfers', because in the previous machine the magnetic drum store had been in a room above the electronics.

So we see that this 'big' machine, which had in part attracted Turing to Manchester, consisted of 256 words of fast memory + 16K words on a (relatively) slow backing store. Nowadays BIG machines have about 1,000,000 words of fast store alone, plus hundreds of millions of words on backing store.

Because of the small size of the machine's memory, Prinz made no attempt to play chess—

> What has been done is a demonstration of the ability of the machine to solve simple chess problems—only the simplest case, the 'mate in two' has been treated, and even so, some of the moves permitted by the rules of chess (double pawn moves, castling and the exchange of a pawn for a piece on reaching the last row) have been excluded to make the programme as simple as possible. Finally, the possibility of a stale mate was admitted as a solution.

The first chess problem solved by the program was the one shown in Fig. 4 (White to move):

This extremely simple problem "took about 15 minutes to solve; most chess players could find the solution in less time than this". Before the reader takes any comfort from this performance by a 25-yr-old machine I should mention that modern machines can, on average, solve mate-in-two problems in about a quarter of a second.

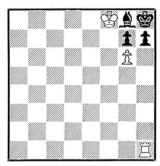

Fig. 4

The above problem was the only one ever solved by the machine—

After establishing that it worked, it was never used again. The number of machine users increased so much that there was not enough time left for frivolities. Besides, any chess problem even slightly more complicated than the one I used would probably have taken hours. In a chess problem, you have to go through all the branches of the trees; you cannot, as in chess playing, ignore the ones not likely to succeed.

One interesting pioneering feature of Prinz's program is that the chess board had an 'edge' to it, i.e. it was actually a 10 × 10 board and, of these 100 squares, only the central 64 constituted the board proper whilst the remaining 36 were used to detect if a piece attempted to move off the board. Unfortunately such a scheme does not prevent a knight making illegal moves; for example, the program would have generated the following for a Black king knight in square 88—(67, 76, 96, **107**? **109**? 100, 80, 69) and only detected 96, 80 and 69 as border squares and hence illegal. When this problem was put to Dr. Prinz (in June 1975) he admitted it was a 'bug' which had not been detected at the time but "it *is* possible to play on a 10 × 10 board provided you split the knight move into two parts: one diagonal, one straight. You would have to test after each part whether the square reached is a border square and, if so, abandon it. Of course, I did not use this technique, it is clumsy and a 10 × 12 board* is much better." I claim this 'bug' as the oldest ever detected.

At the same time as Prinz was writing his chess problem solver, a school teacher from Harrow named Christopher Strachey was programming MADM to play draughts.

* See Chapter 9, Machine Technique.

Strachey had just visited NPL in 1950 to have a look at ACE and find out how it worked 'out of sheer curiosity'. They were still putting it together after 4 years of hard work, but I was able to understand more or less how it was instructed and decided to write a program to play draughts. It so happened that the pilot ACE had a 32-bit word and there are 32 squares on a draughts board. I thought 'How convenient'. As it turned out it was the first draughts program ever written and, as the ACE only had 273 words for data and instructions, it was difficult and damn near killed me because of the need to follow a sequence of captures; just thinking it out and understanding it was very hard but ever since I've always had a clear picture of what recursion is about. Unfortunately the full program never ran—they kept changing the machine—so Mike Woodger suggested that I go to Manchester and try Alan Turing's machine, the Ferranti Mk I. I had known Alan at Kings, Cambridge, before the war and so I asked him to send me a copy of the instruction manual for the machine. He had written the manual himself and when I got a copy I could see why it was famed for its incomprehensibility— people just weren't used to reading really accurate descriptions and this was exacerbated by Alan's slightly irritable assumption that everyone was as intelli- gent as himself. I visited Manchester to find out how MADM worked and then went back to Harrow to write the program. The program was about 19 or 20 'pages' long before I actually tried it. I arrived with it one evening and Turing took me up to the machine room and gave me a quick course on how to use the computer—"You do this, this and this"—and then went away leaving me sat in front of this enormous machine in a room which looked like the control room of a battleship. A quite incredible experience particularly as the machine was, so I believe, worth about £500,000. Fortunately I had the manual and was able to work it out slowly through the night and got most of the program working.

Turing came back in the morning and asked if I had got anywhere and I said 'Oh, yes'. 'Good show' he answered enthusiastically and then told me that the biggest program that had worked so far on the machine was only about half a page, i.e. about 40 times smaller than mine! He made no apologies for letting this fool run in because he believed the only way to really learn how to program was to try problems that were probably too difficult anyway.

The results of Strachey's pioneering work, together with that of Turing and Prinz, are recorded in Bowden's book *Faster than Thought*. Because draughts moves are very much simpler than chess moves it was possible to put both the program and the necessary position storage in the 8 pages of electronic store at the same time thus removing the need for drum transfers 'up' and 'down'. The result was a program that could 'look ahead' 3 plies through all possible alternatives and then make its choice (or mini-max) by valuing the final resulting positions in terms of material left on the board— all this in about 1–2 minutes.

The program could play 'fairly sensibly' but one wholly unexpected difficulty appeared—Strachey discovered what is known as the 'horizon effect', an effect displayed by all programs which search to an *a priori* fixed depth. In chess programs it is most noticeable when an opponent's pawn has reached the seventh rank and is about to queen. This is an enormous gain in his material and, if possible, the program will check the opponent (in both senses) in order to push the evil ply of pawn promotion beyond its look ahead. The trouble is that the checks are usually suicidal and, when all are exhausted, the pawn can often still queen.

In order to avoid this problem Strachey implemented the 'dead position', i.e. the machine continued to investigate moves ahead until it found two consecutive moves without captures. With this strategy the program played a 'tolerable game' until it reached the end game.

After this first program Strachey gave up teaching and went full time into computing, particularly the design of machine languages. He eventually became Professor of Computation at Oxford in 1971 but he never attempted to write a chess program because

> it's too difficult. The name of this game is beating the best chess player in the world and the best program so far is just a box of tricks hiding inside the really incredible development; the general purpose computer. I agree with you that chess programs are an excellent way of investigating what computers can and cannot do but I just happened to find computer languages more interesting and certainly more feasible and worthwhile.

The work of Turing, Prinz and Strachey on MADM put Britain in the lead of chess program development during the early 1950s but this was short-lived. As Prinz has said there was little time for such frivolities and, with the death of Turing, the subject virtually died out at Manchester.

The first chess machine in America was built by Shannon soon after he gave his historic paper. This was a metal cabinet about the size of a tea table and included some 250 relay switches. Named Caissac, after Caissa the goddess of chess, it was very similar to Quevedo's machine in that it could play only the simpler end games, where it had the advantage of a queen, a rook or two bishops. A special chess board, built into the top of the machine, had lights and electrical contacts in each of the squares. It could, therefore, detect where the pieces were and indicated its own moves by flashing the appropriate pair of lights. Unfortunately the algorithms for its play, in particular the king and two bishops vs king, have never been published. Shannon apparently got the message and for the last 20 years has successfully avoided the subject.

The next step forward took place at Los Alamos, New Mexico—an establishment which is not too well known for indulging in frivolities.

It is a fact that the modern electronic computer owes much of its early development to the need to solve the problems of making atomic bombs work. In 1944 the Los Alamos scientists decided that the best solution, indeed the only solution, to assembling a plutonium bomb was to use an imploding lens of conventional explosive. Analytical methods could not simulate how the shock waves would behave in this device and the scientists had to use numerical methods requiring a vast amount of computation (i.e. addition, subtraction, multiplication, etc.). Dr. John von Neumann, then a mathematical consultant to Los Alamos, was ordered to bring into the laboratory the most advanced calculating machines available.

These machines, built by IBM, were electro mechanical and could not be 'programmed' in the modern sense. They were delivered in crates and some curious physicists, unable to wait for the IBM assembly engineers, began putting them together and playing with them. This tendency to play with new, expensive equipment was not discouraged, indeed Dr. Oppenheimer, the Director, appreciated that it was a useful activity. Consequently more machines were ordered and brought in specifically for the physicists to play with, but only in their spare time.

With the successful completion of the first bomb assembly the physicists realised that the new, fully electronic computers, in particular ENIAC, would help to produce smaller, more efficient bombs and, in 1946, von Neumann was given a grant to develop a powerful computer for this purpose. One result of this work was the MANIAC I computer which was installed in Los Alamos about 1950, mainly to study the problems of designing hydrogen bombs.

But the tradition of playing with the computers still continued and in the early 1950s five scientists (including Stanislaw Ulam, the man who had the key to making the hydrogen bomb small enough to carry in a bomber) began to make "some experiments performed on a fast computing machine (MANIAC I—Los Alamos) on the coding of computers to play the game of chess".

The Los Alamos team decided to look 4 plies ahead (2 moves ahead). MANIAC I was fast for its day but it would have taken about 2 hours to consider all possibilities at this depth in the full game.

Consequently a simplified version of chess was used—"we play on a 6 × 6 board, omitting the bishops, and with six pawns on each side. (For the first move we allow the pawn to move only one square ahead.) The game retains much of the flavour of real chess but is very much simpler. Castling is not permitted; promotion of a pawn was allowed to take place as usual."

All this reduced the average time for a move to about 12 minutes. The evaluation of a position was by (material + mobility) with material values as usual (Q=9 pawns, R=5 pawns, etc.) and a pawn was equivalent to 8 legal moves. "These criteria for evaluation seemed to us at the time extremely crude—but—we might say that our simple criteria turned out surprisingly well."

MANIAC I played only three games. In the first game it played itself (White won) and revealed "a mortal fear of checks, since its freedom after check was nearly nil and it tended to sacrifice material to avoid checks".

This, and some other weaknesses, were fixed and the improved program played game 2 against Dr. Martin Kruskal of Princeton University, a strong player who offered it White plus odds of a queen.

The game ran for 10 hours. After about 15 moves Kruskal had made no gain and started calling his opponent 'he' instead of 'it'. At one point MANIAC could have won but it chose badly and Kruskal was able to lay a three-move mating trap. The machine's only way out was to lose its Queen—a decision over which it 'thought' for 20 minutes but "which it did somewhat to the sadness of the authors (and all onlookers but one)". A later official report of the event described the move as 'heartbreaking'.* Kruskal eventually won on his 38th move.

The third game was against a young lady who had no knowledge of chess. She was coached for a week and then, playing Black, became the first human to lose a game of chess to a machine.

At move 18 she was faced with (Fig. 5)

Fig. 5

* The COKO incident is even more heartbreaking. See Chapter 5.

and played P–Q3. MANIAC now demonstrated that if 'he' was male then
he was a male chauvenist and, showing no chivalry, played

19	N–R3+	K–K1
20	P–N5+	K–K2
21	P×R(Q)	N–Q2
22	Q×P+	K–Q1
23	N–N5++	

And so "with very little in the way of complexity, we have at least entered
the arena of human play—we can beat a beginner".

The full 64-square game was tried later (*ca.* 1956) on a faster machine,
MANIAC II, and achieved comparable results.

The next program of note was developed about 1956 by Alex Bernstein,
a mathematician and strong amateur player. The machine used was an
IBM 704 which was capable of about 10,000 instructions (add, subtract,
compare, etc.) per second, i.e. about 10 times faster than MADM but still
1000 times slower than modern machines.

Bernstein's program was, in both senses, extremely curious—it spent
almost half its time asking questions (mainly because it had forgotten the
answer). For example: "The computer painstakingly and single-mindedly
considers square by square, giving the same minute attention to squares of
little interest as to those of key importance. It asks about each square
whether it is occupied, by whose man, whether it is attacked, whether it is
defended, whether it can be occupied."

All this took about one-tenth of a second and was repeated in the look
ahead over 2400 times—and usually obtaining the answer 'no'. Personally
I am not fond of this idea, the program asked too many irrelevant questions whereas the art of programming is simple command—the machine
should 'do it' until a limiting or satisfactory condition is reached.

The reason Bernstein's program asked these and other questions is that
it had a very restricted depth and width. It could only search four plies
ahead and only consider (at most) seven alternatives at each ply. To choose
the seven alternatives the program had what is now termed a 'seven
plausible moves selector'. It picked these moves on the basis of a further
eight questions. First it asked

(1) Am I in check? If so list only appropriate moves, i.e. capture checking piece, block or move the king. If not in check then

(2) Are any exchanges possible? If so can I gain material or should I move my man away.

The questions continue:

(3) If I have not castled, can I do so now?

(4) Can I develop a bishop or knight?

(5) Can I occupy an open file?

(6) Can I place pieces on critical squares of my pawn structure?

(7) Can I make a pawn move?

(8) Can I make a piece move?

The machine asked these questions in the above order until it has found a maximum of seven plausible moves. Repeating the process to a depth of four plies resulted in ·2401 possible positions which were evaluated by gain of material, defence of king, mobility and control of central squares. The best value was backed up the tree and the machine made its moves; the time taken for all this was about 8 minutes.

The program was punched on about 8000 cards which were fed into the machine. In order to play the machine one had to punch a move on a card, put this card into a reader and press the start button. The machine's reply was output on a lineprinter.

Despite the fact that Bernstein's program now appears a poor approach —wasting a great deal of its allotted time asking questions and the input/output of moves was archaic—it was this program that first played "a respectable and not-too-obvious game of chess" Edward Lasker, the American chess master and author, played the machine twice. The first game was more of an investigation; Lasker tested the program by putting six of his men *en prise*—they could all be taken if the program was 'smart' enough to capture them in the correct order. He lost them all. Lasker then played a second time to win and did so inside 20 moves but (he later said) the program played a 'passable amateur game' and with bigger, more powerful machines "quite a strong game could be produced—without changing its method in principle".

All these first programs were 'brute-force' programs which, apart from Bernstein's, made little or no pretence to simulate what happens in a good chess player's mind. One strikingly common feature of these prototype experiments is that all the authors—Prinz, Strachey, Ulam and Bernstein—stated roughly the same conclusion:

"It appears that if this crude method of programming were the only one available it would be quite impractical for any machine to compete on reasonable terms with a competent human being."

Lord Bowden on Prinz

"It's too difficult."

Strachey

"It is clear that even much faster machines—having, say, one microsecond order times will not enable one to look more than 3 moves ahead", i.e. 6 plies in their simplified version

Ulam et al.

"Even with much faster computers than any now in existence it will be impracticable to consider more than about six half moves ahead, investigating eight possible moves at each stage."

Bernstein

So despite all these successes (between 1951 and 1956), there was a distinct pessimism on the subject by people who had actually got the programs to work. This pessimism was to last for a decade awaiting the discovery of the alpha–beta principle.

CHAPTER 5

The Crunchers

IT IS not quite true to say that everyone who had written a chess program before 1957 was pessimistic. There was an attempt to write a program which would simulate more closely human chess-playing methods and the authors of this program were rather more hopeful.

This was a research project by Herbert Simon, Allen Newell and Clifford Shaw of the Rand Corporation and the Carnegie Institute of Technology. Their program was very complex, very slow—it could take an hour over a move—and none of its games was ever published. Simon summarised (in 1957): "Our program is fairly impressive in the very opening play when center control and development are at issue. I think at this stage we can rate it at the medium amateur level (about 1200 ELO rating or 75 British). But after that, it isn't so good." Nevertheless Simon was uniquely optimistic, he believed "that within 10 years a digital computer will be the world's chess champion, unless the rules bar it from competition".

Well the years passed by and there were only a few desultory twitches in the subject. An American machine played a Russian machine (and lost), Barbara Huberman appeared to show that simple end games were horribly difficult for computers (this is dealt with more fully in Chapter 7) but, and this was probably the biggest hold up, the new, more powerful computers were no longer dedicated to one program and it was difficult to 'talk' to a program without making the machine 'inefficient', i.e. it would have to wait for its opponent's moves and this idling was anathema to the new half-breed of computer managers. Chess programs became *programma non grata* in the new, batch mode computer systems.

We now come to what is known in the subject as 'the Dreyfus Affair'.

In 1965 Professor Hubert Dreyfus was aware of Simon's optimistic statement of 1957. Simon had later re-evaluated the MANIAC II program at Los Alamos, the IBM 704 program of Bernstein and his own, and come to the more pessimistic (and realistic) conclusion that all three programs played mediocre chess. Nevertheless Dreyfus could not resist commenting on Simon's previous optimism: "Still no chess program can play even amateur chess, and the world championship is only 2 years away."

This comment in *Phenomonology and Artificial Intelligence* was part of an attack on Artificial Intelligence in general. Dreyfus used the failure of chess programs in particular to make his case and plainly gave the impression that such programs could be defeated by novices, even 10-year-old novices.

Unfortunately for Dreyfus a new chess program was just being developed at the Massachusett's Institute of Technology and he was invited to play it. The A.I. newsletter SIGART reprinted the game with no comment other than ". . . no chess program can play even amateur chess . . ."— Hubert L. Dreyfus, Dec. 1965.

	White (Dreyfus)	*Black (Program)*
1	P–K4	P–K4
2	N–KB3	N–QB3
3	B–B4	N–B3
4	N–B3	B–B4
5	P–Q3	0–0
6	N–KN5	N–QR4
7	B–Q5	P–B3
8	B–N3	N×B
9	BP×N	P–KR3
10	N–R3	P–Q4
11	P×P	B–KN5
12	P–B3	B×N
13	P×B	N×P
14	N×N	Q×N
15	B–Q2	Q×QP
16	P–N4	B–K2
17	R–KN1	P–K5
18	P×P	B–R5+
19	R–N3	B×R+
20	P×B	Q×NP+
21	K–K2	Q×P
22	Q–KN1	P–KR4

White (*Dreyfus*)		Black (*Program*)
23	B–B3	P–KN3
24	Q–B2	P–R5
25	Q–B6	Q–N5+
26	K–Q2	QR–Q1+
27	K–B2	Q×P+
28	K–N3	Q–K3+
29	Q×Q	P×Q
30	R–R1	R–B5
31	B–K1	R–B6+
32	K–R4	P–R6
33	P–N5	R–Q5+
34	P–N4	P×P+
35	K×P	R–R6
36	K–B5	R–Q4+
37	K–B4	P–N4++

Of course all that this game proved (to quote Professor Seymour Papert of the MIT Artificial Intelligence Group) was that "Computers Can't Play Chess—Nor Can Dreyfus" and everyone involved had a good laugh—well almost everyone!

Dreyfus protested that he had been quoted out of context, complained of such tactics being used to discredit his arguments and repeated his criticism of the over-optimism of chess programmers.

This debate, in one form or another, continues to the present day but where Dreyfus went wrong is that he implied that *all* chess programmers were over-optimistic. This is not, nor ever was, the case for the majority of people who have written chess programs—generally these people are either non-commital or extremely pessimistic as to when a computer will be world champion* and it is only a small faction that have caused problems and gained fame by irresponsible predictions.

The program that had beaten Dreyfus was called MACHACK and was written by Richard Greenblatt and Donald Eastlake. Apart from Dreyfus the program had played in a few local tournaments in the period February to May 1967 and had actually won a trophy in April. Against non-tournament players MACHACK could win about 80 per cent of its games.

---

* At the 1974 Computer Chess World Championship the majority of opinion was 1983+ for a master chess program and probably never for a world champion.

There were four main reasons for MACHACK's success. First: Greenblatt and Eastlake were competent, pragmatic programmers and not just paper theorists. Second: as Greenblatt says, "The environment in which this program has been developed is, we feel, more advantageous than for any previous chess program." What he meant here was that he had a dedicated, highly interactive machine (a PDP–6) with good software facilities for editing and debugging the program which itself was written in a high-level assembly language. Third: the alpha–beta principle was used to reduce the work by a factor of about 100. Finally: people who played the program would resign prematurely. They did not realise that although MACHACK was impressive in the opening and middle game, it was often incapable of winning quite simple end games.

Because it was written in a high-level language it was possible to give MACHACK a much more sophisticated 'plausible-move generator' containing about fifty conditions for choosing moves for further investigation. The numbers of plausible moves (the 'width of search') were variable and, for tournament play, were set to 15 at ply 1, 15 at ply 2, 9 at ply 3, 9 at ply 4 and finally 7 at ply 5.

At ply 5 the program applied its 'evaluation' of the position. If captures were present, i.e. the position was not 'dead', then the program could recall the plausible-move generator to go deeper providing the line was forced.

Having evaluated a position as quiescent or dead the program would give it a 'value of the board', S, which was again quite complex:

$$S = \text{material balance} + \text{piece ratio} + \text{pawn structure} + \text{king safety} + \text{center control.}$$

Material balance was, as usual, the dominant term and was calculated from the following piece values:

Piece	Value	Value relative to pawn
Pawn	128	1
Knight	416	3·25
Bishop	448	3·50
Rook	640	5
Queen	1248	9.75
King	1536	12

N.B. The loss of, for example, a queen and knight was considered equivalent to losing the game.

The piece ratio term was probably the first attempt to make a program take even or near even exchanges when ahead and avoid them when behind—incidentally, a piece of advice which Dreyfus had not followed in his game with the program.

The pawn structure gave (or took off) points for passed, isolated, backward and doubled pawns; pawns also increased in value as they advanced being roughly equivalent to a minor piece at the seventh rank.

The king safety term only applied when queens were on the board and was (eight times the rank of the Black king minus eight times the rank of the White king). The program's king was therefore reluctant to move from the back rank whilst the opponent's queen was still in play.

Centre control was probably the weakest part of the program because it inhibited the program from moving pawns out of the centre four squares *even in the end game.*

The resulting 'value of the board' was then mini-maxed back up the tree, with alpha–beta cutoff, and MACHACK chose its move.

Despite having a fair amount of 'chess knowledge', nobody claimed (least of all Greenblatt) that the program thought like a human player. As Shannon had advised, MACHACK derived most of its power from its lookahead in a machine capable of 200,000 operations per second. But it was a powerful opening and middle game player with the ability to fool people into thinking that it 'knew' what it was doing in an intelligent activity.

In 1967 this ability was not unique, a number of programs had by then appeared which could fool people or make it difficult for them to know whether they were interacting with a machine or another human. There was, for example, a draughts (checkers) playing program which, because the game is much simpler, could play up to almost world champion level. Another program (called ELIZA) was even more bizarre in that it could apparently carry on a conversation. Basically this program never volunteered any information but either asked a question or made a sympathetic, understanding comment.

In the 1940s Turing had considered the question of whether a machine could *be said to be* 'thinking'. Turing wrote that the answer is essentially subjective and invented the Turing test to illustrate the point.

In the Turing test a human investigator is sat at a teletype on which he can type anything he likes and something (either another human or a machine) will type back a response. If the investigator cannot tell whether the responses are from another human or a machine then, by any sensible definition, the responder is 'thinking'.

In 1968 a student went into the AI office at MIT to use one of the on-line teletypes. One of these appeared to be free but had a note "Computer time reserved by Dan Bobrow". The student sat down and linked to Bobrow's home terminal (so he thought, he actually linked to ELIZA) with the following conversation:

STUDENT: MAY I USE YOUR COMPUTER TIME?
: DO YOU WANT TO USE MY COMPUTER TIME?
STUDENT: YES.
: I UNDERSTAND.
STUDENT: ARE YOU COMING IN TONIGHT?
: WHY DO YOU WANT TO KNOW IF I AM COMING IN TONIGHT?
STUDENT: BECAUSE I WANT TO USE THE COMPUTER!!!
: I SEE.
STUDENT: WELL?
WHAT DO YOU MEAN, "WELL"?
STUDENT: WELL, WHAT'S YOUR ANSWER?
: LET'S EXPLORE FURTHER WHY YOU WANT TO USE THE COMPUTER.

After a further 10 minutes of increasing frustration the student rushed to a telephone and dialled Bobrow's home, rousing him from a deep sleep.

STUDENT: WHAT THE HECK DO YOU THINK YOU'RE DOING?
BOBROW: WHAT DO YOU MEAN, WHAT THE HECK DO I THINK I'M DOING?

So at least one program had passed the Turing test with flying colours. Now Greenblatt's program had also passed the test for the simple reason that people would resign against it; it obviously convinced some people that it 'knew' what it was doing.

MACHACK was not a breakthrough but it did herald a breakout of chess programs. Between 1967 and 1970 at least eight new programs appeared in the United States and, from 31 August to 2 September 1970 there occurred, in connection with the Association of Computing Machinery (ACM) Convention in New York, the first United States Computer Chess Championship.

Six programs competed in the event and it was won by a program written by David Slate, Larry Atkin and Keith Gorlen of Northwestern University. Their program, CHESS 3.0 won all its three games.

The following year eight programs competed in Chicago in another three-round 'Swiss Tournament' and again CHESS 3.5 won all its games—and again in 1972. CHESS 3.6 had by then run up a perfect record of nine consecutive victories although it was finding it more difficult to knock out its opponents.

One of its games in the ACM-1972 tournament at Boston is of particular interest because Samuel Reshevsky, a master player and former U.S. Title Holder, published an analysis in the *New York Times.** Note CHESS 3.6's style of pawn wrecking.

The relevant part of the game is as follows:

	Slate/Atkin Northwestern University *CDC* 6400 CHESS 3.6	James Gillogly Carnegie–Mellon *PDP*–10 TECH
1	P–K4	P–K4
2	N–KB3	N–QB3
3	B–N5	N–B3
4	0–0	B–B4
5	N–B3	P–Q3
6	B×N+	P×B
7	P–Q4	P×P
8	N×P	0–0
9	B–N5	B–KN5
10	Q–Q3	B×N
11	Q×B	R–N1
12	B×N	Q×B
13	Q×Q	P×Q
14	P–QN3	R–N5
15	P–KR3	B–K3
16	P–N4	R–Q5
17	QR–Q1	R×R
18	N×R	K–N2
19	N–K3	K–N3
20	P–KB4	K–N2
21	K–N2	R–QN1
22	K–B3	R–N4
23	P–B4	R–QR4

* "Analysis Puts Fischer Ahead of IBM", 18 August 1972.

Slate/Atkin	James Gillogly
Northwestern University	Carnegie–Mellon
CDC 6400	*PDP*–10
CHESS 3.6	TECH
24 P–KB5	B–Q2
25 R–B2	R–K4
26 R–Q2	P–QR3
27 P–KR4	P–B4?

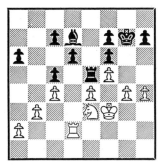

Fig. 7

28 N–Q5	B–B3
29 N×QBP	B×P+
30 K–B4	P–KR4
31 P×P	P–R4
32 R×P	B×P
33 P–R6+	K–N3
34 P–R5+	K×P/4
35 R×P	R–K7
36 K×B	—

Reshevsky's analysis:

The computer chess match in Boston proved one thing: computers have a long way to go before they become international grandmasters. But their game was an interesting experiment nonetheless.

Black's reply on the ninth move of . . . B–KN5 was amazing. But TECH had calculated that its move was not a blunder.

It must be realised that if 10 B×N, Q×B, then: 11 Q×B, B×N, with a playable game. And when White concluded it would not profit from the above continuation, it correctly continued 10 Q–Q3.

On the 11 move, TECH allowed its opponent to break up its king pawn position. Prudent was 11 . . . P–B3 (instead of R–N1) and if CHESS 3.6 persisted

in its apparently intended continuation of 12 B×N, then 12 . . . P×Q; 13 B×Q
P×N 14 B×P P×P 15 QR–N1 KR–B1 16 B×P R×P, with an even position.
But that was really too much to expect from a computer.

TECH was saddled with two doubled pawns in the end game. Chess 3.6
pressed its advantage reasonably well.

CHESS 3.6 displayed good judgement on its 18th turn when it recaptured the
rook with its knight instead of its own rook, realising that the knight could be
better utilised at K3 than at QB3.

White's 20 P–KB4 was a mechanical but useful stroke. It threatened to win the
bishop with P–B5ch, and TECH, seeing it, moved its king away.

White's 25th move, R–B2, protected his* queen rook pawn. How did CHESS
3.6 ever see that it was attacked by Black's rook? TECH slipped on its 27th move
when it advanced its queen bishop pawn. Correct was 27 . . . P–R3 with an even
position.

White's 28th move, N–Q5, was a star move for a computer. Black's position
was untenable from here on. TECH's 30 . . . P–KR4 was a good try but insufficient.

White's 33 P–KR6ch, on the other hand, was a computer stroke of genius!
Of course, 33 . . . K×P; 34 R×Pch would have finished it off right there. White
was really concentrating when it played 34 P–R5ch.

After 35 R×P, TECH could have resigned, but being a good computer it
fought until the bitter end.

In December 1972, Jack Good (the Bletchley statistical assistant of
Turing) had the temerity to comment on Reshevsky's analysis. At move 27
Black played P–B4 "and Reshevsky says that 27 P–R3 would have given an
even position. This seems undeniable for current chess programs, but it
seems to me that White has an objectively won position." Basically what
Good proposed was that the White knight could win the KB pawn via
N–N2–B4–R5+.

This comment was published in SIGART in February 1973 with an
Editor's Note: "I wrote a letter to Mr. Reshevsky, enclosing the correspondence (of Dr. Good) and saying, 'It is alleged that "27 P–R3" does
not yield an even position as you said earlier but, assuming this is true, I
don't believe you should be faulted for not realising that White may still
have a winning advantage. After all, it was a position that occurred in the
middle of a uniformly poor game (by master standards)'."

It is a curious note—I have never been sure exactly who or what is being
insulted—however Reshevsky replied (coldly) that he disagreed that the
White knight could capture the pawn: "Black can defend the KBP
with 28 . . . K–B1, and if 29 N–(B4)–R5, Black continues . . . K–K2.
Secondly, after 28 N–N2, Black equalises with 28 . . . P–KR4 29 P–N5
P×P 30 P×P P–Q4, etc. P.S. Until you can engage a Grandmaster of

* The best chess programs are all masculine eventually.

high repute, the computer will never get anywhere. Samuel Reshevsky
NEW YORK."

Meanwhile, down in Virginia and unaware of Reshevsky's response,
Jack Good continued his investigation until 1 month after his first comment: "I now believe Reshevsky was right, in view of the following
line:

27 ... P–KR3   28 N–N2 P–KR4   29 N–B4 P×P+   30 K–N3 K–R3
31 R–K2 R–K1.

"It would be interesting to know if Reshevsky saw all this or whether he
just used his judgement."

So much for what is probably still the most carefully analysed position
in the history of computer chess, but the affair was not yet over. Hans
Berliner, three times World Correspondence Chess Champion, was moved
to make a 'meta comment' as follows:

> Though I usually prefer to smile (benignly) when chess amateurs discuss
> computer problems, the discussion in the SIGART Newsletter of February 1973
> was a little too much for me.
>
> First of all, I would think that Mr. Good would know better than to challenge
> the judgement of Mr. Reshevsky when it comes to chess. I am sure Mr. Reshevsky
> would have the good sense not to get into a statistics debate with Mr. Good.
>
> Secondly, such positions should be analysed for the general public at a level
> commensurate with the play of the competitors in the game. To measure the
> outcome of a position by grandmaster standards when Class C players are
> involved is ludicrous. It is done only in tournaments when a game cannot be
> finished and must be adjudicated, and I wince every time I am called upon to do
> that.
>
> Thirdly, Mr. Fischer* and Mr. Reshevsky should be informed that chess players
> of great reputation and ability are working on the chess programming problem.
> They may not want to include me, since their joint over the board score against
> me is 6½–½. However, the credentials of Dr. M. M. Botvinnik of the Soviet Union
> are impeccable. Besides being probably the greatest player of all times (unless
> now eclipsed by Fischer), he has outstanding contributions credited to him in the
> field of electrical engineering. Further, I think all persons interested in chess
> programming ought to be informed that for any of today's chess programs, it
> would be impossible to encode 90 per cent of what I know about chess. The
> problem is the usual semantic data base problem.

Now Berliner's second point had, in all fairness, been made by Good
already, i.e. the position in question was 'objectively won'. Both men were
aware that chess programs were, and still are, notorious for throwing away

---

* "Up till now they've only had computer scientists developing such programs, and
they won't get anywhere until they actually involve some good chess players." Bobby
Fischer, December, 1972.

a won game. The most famous example of this predeliction had occurred in the ACM Tournament of 1971.

The Coko Incident

In a game between COKO III and GENIE this position was reached after 27 moves.

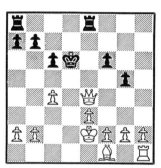

Fig. 8

After 120 seconds' calculation, COKO offered a sacrificial pawn to pull the Black king out further:

28   P–B5+   K×P

In fact COKO had looked ahead 8½ moves and seen the following mating sequence which it now played very quickly:

29   Q–Q4+   K–N4

(this move took 3 seconds and COKO, because of Black's K×P, had already announced the mate. The next 8 moves of COKO took less than 1 second to be retrieved from its memory.)

30	K–Q1+	K–R4
31	P–N4+	K–R5
32	Q–B3	KR–Q1+
33	K–B2	R–Q7+
34	K×R	R–Q1+
35	K–B2	R–Q7+
36	Q×R	K–R6

At this point GENIE had thrown away two rooks to delay the inevitable. No further distractions or delays were possible

37   Q–B3+   K×P

As Reshevsky said, good computers fight to the bitter end, and here's the reason why:

38	K–B1	P–KB4
39	K–B2	P–B5
40	K–B1	P–N5
41	K–B2	P–B6
42	K–B1	P×P
43	K–B2	P×R = Q

Do it now!? No way, like the hero of *The Loneliness of the Long Distance Runner*, COKO proves it has a mind of its own:

44   K–B1 and GENIE plods firmly back into the game . . .

		Q×B+
45	K–Q2	Q×P+
46	K–B1	Q–N8+
47	K–B2	Q×P+
48	K–B1	Q–R8+
49	K–B2	Q–N8+
50	K–Q2	P–N6
51	Q–B4+	Q–N6
52	Q×Q	K×Q
53	P–K4	K×P
54	P–K5	P–N7

At this point COKO's authors, Dennis Cooper and Ed Kozdrowicki, could stand it no longer and the program was resigned. After COKO's display many people would have said the game was subjectively drawn at this point; GENIE would have queened its pawn and then probably have spent the next 100 or so moves making irrelevant checks. In a later paper Cooper and Kozdrowicki admitted that "In early stages of development, COKO was actually winning games from casual players who did not realise that (it) was unable to mate with a Queen and a Rook against a King in endgame." This phenomena of playing very good middle games and then being unable to win a simple end game is still typical of most chess programs and has a simple explanation—end games are highly specialised and require hundreds of hours for humans to become competent. Computers are not specialised and it can cost £1000 per hour to run a program so the best thing is to try for a big tactical advantage in the middle game and thus avoid the more subtle specialities of end games.

This approach was, and still is, the overall strategy adopted by Slate and Atkin when writing CHESS 4.0.

To return to the ACM tournaments. The fourth took place at Atlanta, Georgia, in August 1973. The winner was (as usual) CHESS 4.0; a completely rewritten version which nevertheless showed its usual workmanlike style by messing up its opponent's pawns, advancing its own pawns and even playing out some simple end games to a win.

Admittedly the competition appeared to be improving (very slightly) because CHESS 4.0 finished this tournament with three wins and a draw, thus slightly blotting its perfect run. Still it was (and is) a remarkably consistent program and, in 1974, it entered the first World Computer Chess Championship as clear favourite to win. But this championship had a number of dark horses, notably the Russian program KAISSA. There was also a program from England, the birthplace of computer chess, whose name was MASTER.

CHAPTER 6

MASTER at IFIPS

This chapter is the story of how a poor but honest chess program eventually played in the World Championship.

In 1954 Professor Nils Barricelli was visiting Princeton University. The University was then a leader in the new field of computing mainly due to the presence of von Neumann and his development of the (amongst others) MANIAC machines.

In a discussion with Reuben Fine, the well-known Grandmaster and psychologist, Barricelli said that he intended to program a machine in order to beat Fine in chess. "Professor Fine replied that he was sure the machine would play a poor game. Whereupon we asked von Neumann of his opinion. He agreed with Professor Fine on the grounds that the machine was not even capable of translating from a foreign language into a decent English.* I think that was a poor argument, but that was anyhow his opinion."

In 1962 Barricelli arrived at Manchester University in order to use the Atlas computer, a machine with many new features and probably, at the time, the most powerful computer in the world. His intention was to write a chess program which would be used to study certain theories of evolution.

I was at Manchester at the time having just finished a year of computer research. Having also just got married I had turned my attention to the mundane problems of earning a living and was told that a Dr. Barry Chelly was looking for someone to write a chess program for Atlas. My first job ever was to help write a 'list legal moves' generator for any chess position on a machine which was barely operational.

Cooper and Kozdrowicki have remarked that "chess will persist, for the

---

* Von Neumann could speak five languages fluently. Even more important—the remark is extremely relevant—chess has a language, a game is a conversation of a kind.

problem is so exciting that once a programmer gets involved there is virtually no way he can be stopped". Personally I do not agree but I do remember that working with Barricelli was an interesting experience which definitely sold me on a career in computing although Manchester was an exciting place for computer users in almost any subject at the time.

The legal-move generator had to be as fast as possible because it would be used by symbio-organisms—numerical patterns in the machine which could reproduce and mutate—to test evolutionary theories. In order to survive and grow* these organisms had to learn how to play chess; this was their test in their battle for survival.

At the time we did consider making the program play a game against a human (though I would stress that this was not the aim of the project). Without reference to any literature we wrote a Shannon–Turing lookahead (it is a very obvious model) and an evaluation function based purely on mobility. We spent a whole week on this and the results were discouraging —we could beat it easily. Nevertheless it was a useful program for testing the, then, very new Atlas and on one occasion it ran silent and deep for 20 minutes before making its opening move, P–K4.

At the time this was probably the first fully legal chess program to run in England (possibly the world) but Barricelli's grant ran out and, seeing no pecuniary future in the subject, I went off to earn a living doing something useful. I was, however, left with the naïve impression that a chess program could be built in three separate parts, namely: (a) list legal moves; (b) look ahead; (c) an evaluation function.

For the next 5 years I worked on systems at the Atlas Computer Laboratory, mainly developing and extending an Algol Compiler. In 1967 it at last became possible to go 'on-line' to a program in the machine and I resurrected Barricelli's old program, cleaned it up, rewrote it in ALGOL and put it on the machine.

This version was mainly a demonstration program for the new on-line console. Much of the effort went into producing an agreeable input/output system—for example, the program would ask what colour the opponent wanted, type 'EH?' if he entered an illegal move, output its own move in descriptive form and, if required, print the current position of the board. Its strategy was simple, it looked only 3 plies ahead and would accept almost any captures in that depth with weighting on swaps of the more

---

* In early tests the organisms actually invaded the private parts of the machine and halted it.

powerful pieces, i.e. it would always swap a queen for a queen. If no captures were present it prepared to castle or mini-maximised its mobility. A slight modification prevented it from moving its queen in the first 5 moves.

This program, although written in ALGOL, used the alpha–beta principle and could respond almost immediately to the moves of the opponent —and it was fairly pathetic. One of its first games was against Lord Halsbury, a weak player but one who knew how to get at a king side castled position—his Black queen went to KN3 and then his bishop went to KR6—it was all over in 20 moves.

Nevertheless I felt that this strategy of capturing as often as possible would fare quite well against other chess programs. Even in 1968 it was quite obvious that chess programs could win massive material advantages and still not 'know' what to do—MACHACK had clearly shown this failing on occasion.

The only other chess program in England in 1968 was one written by John Scott, then a 17-year-old schoolboy. His program actually played MACHACK at the Edinburgh IFIPS (International Federation of Information Processing) and just lost after a long struggle (see also Chapter 8). John and I were present at a talk a few days later by Jack Good who analysed this game; in fact, we both remember that some of the reasons given for John's program choosing a move were, in our opinion, over-sophisticated.

John and I arranged to play our programs against each other. I was interested to see how the simple strategy of attrition at 3 plies would fare against a more sophisticated program. Only two games were possible because neither program could learn or randomise equal possibilities. Here is one of them

	SCOTT	ATLAS	
1	P–Q4	N–QB3	attacks pawn
2	P–K4	P–K3	mobility
3	P–Q5	B–N5+	horizon effect
4	P–QB3	B–B4	mobility
5	P–QN4	N×P	best capture
6	P×N	Q–B3	horizon effect
7	P×B	Q×R	
8	B–Q3	Q×P	
9	N–KB3	P×P	inevitable

SCOTT   ATLAS

10	P×P	Q×P	
11	N–B3	Q×P	
12	B–Q2	N–B3	prepare 0–0

It is a silly game with ATLAS clearly suffering from the horizon effect at moves 3 and 6. Despite this SCOTT does not take full advantage, it failed to develop any pieces until move 8 and consequently got itself into trouble.

So at the end of 1968 I was fairly sure that chess programs might fool some people some of the time but they really could not know, in any real sense, what they were doing, mainly because they were too shortsighted. Almost any chess player, provided he kept his nerve and never resigned, could—by following a simple plan of swapping off—almost guarantee that even MACHACK would not beat him.

So once again I went off to do something useful—to Paris this time where I finally learnt that any talent for writing programs has very little to do with the brave, new world of computers.

In 1972 I was back in England again and met John Scott, who was doing a PhD, and his tutor Dr. Alan Bond. Naturally we talked about chess programs and the recent happenings in the American ACM tournaments. As we talked it became fairly obvious that in the intervening 4 years a number of new ideas had appeared on the scene. One idea was called 'refutation', a technique which (like alpha–beta) could vastly speed up the tree searching without any loss of information (see Chapter 9—Machine Technique).

Even more mysterious was a paper "Multi Dimensional Structure in the Game of Chess" by Ron Atkin, a maths lecturer at Essex University. Up to this point all chess programs had evaluation functions which were decidedly *ad hoc*, the programmers had a 'feeling in their water' that certain features, material, mobility, control of the centre, king safety, pawn structure, etc., were the most important and accordingly stuck them in the program with very little idea of their precise effect. Now here was a mathematician who, with lots of squiggly things, appeared to have a precise mathematical evaluation function. Unfortunately neither John nor I could understand the paper—so why not get Atkin to talk about it. There were a few other new ideas I did not understand—a new, knowledge approach to solving end games and some psychological theories about how

Plate 1. Torres y Quevedo's chess machine (see Chapter 2).

Plate 2. The author's daughter playing a modern chess machine.

Plate 3. The author and son Richard outside Ramon Lull's cave
on Mount Randa (see Chapter 7).

Plate 4. The MASTER team. Left to right: The author, Peter Kent, John Birmingham and John Waldron.

chess players think—so why not have a conference? If nothing else I might get some idea of what was going on.

The first Computer Chess Conference took place at the Atlas Computer Laboratory in May 1973. Apart from inviting the speakers it was also obvious that the conference would have to demonstrate a chess program in some form and it is at this point in time that MASTER really got started.

I had left my old program purely as an on-line demonstration.* Its evaluation was based simply on capturing plus mobility and, although it worked to a certain extent, had two noticeable weaknesses: (1) no value was given to an undeveloped piece, such as a rook or bishop, and (2) the queen tended to come out too soon. These faults, combined with the horizon effect caused by a too shallow search, made the program very weak; in fact it never beat anybody. One of the programmers at Atlas, Peter Kent, had taken over the program and modified it to maximise the number of squares controlled. This, combined with a few other improvements, had produced a much stronger program—as Peter later wrote

> The program captured if you gave it the chance, moved a piece if threatened, but still generally displayed no imagination. The computer operators used to play the program at night and write sarcastic comments on the output after winning in 15 or so moves. I then decided to try building some sort of strategy into the program by giving the squares different values. Initially the ratios were 3 for the central four squares, 2 for the next ring of twelve and 1 for all the remainder.
>
> The next night the best player among the operators tried playing the program expecting to win with his usual ease. The program opened with the rather aggressive if unsound Blackmar gambit. It then developed all its pieces fairly rapidly, castled queen side, doubled its rooks on the open queen file and stormed down the board using both rooks and the queen, ending the game with a mate by its queen on the 8th rank and a rook on the 7th. The comment on the output the next morning was "well it seems to work now".

From then on the operators played more carefully and revealed that the program, because it still only had a shallow search, still suffered badly from horizon effect. Nevertheless it did win a few more games and it was decided to use it as the demonstration program at the conference.

Well it didn't win a game, hardly surprising since it was up against much stronger players. Nevertheless several people noticed that the program was usually achieving its main aim of controlling the centre squares; in other words, it was quite successful in doing what little it had been told

---

* Getting a program 'on line' is, even now, quite difficult but this fact was usually not appreciated—after all chess programs only play chess and are misjudged accordingly.

to do but, from then on, it had no further direction other than a vague idea of advancing its own pawns and blocking its opponent's. Peter improved its sense of purpose by making the program, as the game progressed, put less emphasis on controlling the fixed centre squares and more and more emphasis on controlling the squares around the enemy king, wherever he may be. Because of mini–max this also caused the program to protect the squares around its own king far more effectively.

This change from centre control to actively hunting the opponent's king was very noticeable. At this point a very energetic programmer from Harwell Atomic Energy Research Establishment, John Birmingham, became interested. He translated the program, plus all the new improvements, into PL/1 in about 6 weeks of his spare time and also extended the depth of the search. I would say at this point that England at last had a program comparable to MACHACK and we ambitiously christened it MASTER—*M*inimax *A*lgorithm te*STER*; if nothing else we had the patent on a good name.

In March 1974 David Levy, the regular referee and one of the organisers of the American ACM tournaments, rang me up—did I know of any good English chess programs? And, if so, would they like to enter the first IFIPS World Computer Chess Championship which would take place at Stockholm in August? So MASTER was entered, and for the first time we—John, Peter and myself—stopped developing the program sporadically *ad hoc* and seriously thought about how to improve it. One big problem was that none of us was (or is) a good chess player and by then the program was beginning to beat us occasionally.

So a fourth member of the team was recruited—John Waldron, a sound county level player. From this point MASTER slowly began to copy Waldron's style and, with the program now searching 6 plies deep plus a crude form of a new technique (feedover), it took part in the first World Championship.

To take part in a World Championship a contestant merely has to arrive on time. This is comparatively easy for humans (except maybe Bobby Fischer) but much more difficult for computers.

For a start, computers—especially the really big ones—work 24 hours a day, 7 days a week to pay for their keep. In MASTER's case we could only get a total of 2 hours sabbatical leave (in an IBM 360/195) for it to take part. Another problem is that computers do not travel well and are usually linked to the tournament by telephone or teletypes. Finally computers do occasionally 'crash', i.e. stop working, and the rules allow only 20 minutes to recover from such situations and continue the game. All these problems are time problems which require a great deal of preparation to overcome—the program, the links, the machine and the recovery procedures must all be as fast and as dependable as possible; if not then the program's actual chess ability can count for nothing. (Many chess programmers know more about recovery techniques than the resident systems analysts.)

MASTER's first game took place on the evening of 4 August 1974 and, to emphasise the peripheral problems, we were 1 hour late in establishing the link between our computer (in Oxfordshire, England) and Stockholm. When we did get through, at 20.30 the first thing we asked was what was the opponent—we had a vague idea that if it was CHESS 4.0 then we would risk the time limits and make MASTER search wider and longer than usual.

The opponent was TECH 2, however, another American program with a steady, plodding nature, so MASTER was set to play fast (at about 45 seconds per move) and started as White.

MASTER opened with the King's Gambit and soon sacrificed a knight a la MUZIO for heavy pressure. TECH 2 gave up its queen for a further rook and bishop and, by move 40, the game had simplified (!?) to the following position (Fig. 8).

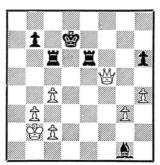

Fig. 8

By this time it was midnight and MASTER had used up its quarter ration of half an hour's machine time. We had the mistaken idea that an adjudication was automatic at the completion of 40 moves and requested one from the tournament referee David Levy. Not only were we mistaken about the

40-move limit but Levy said (correctly!) that if we did not continue then he would award the decision to TECH 2.

Convinced that the position was 'objectively' drawn we stoked up the machine and ran on for another 48 moves. Unfortunately MASTER disagreed with us, it believed it was winning the game and disdained a draw by perpetual check (it would have done this if it thought it was losing). The final outcome was that TECH 2 eventually co-ordinated its pieces, broke through and gave mate.

TECH'S most infuriating habit in this game derived from its steady, plodding nature, it always took the same time over every move—even if the move was forced—so the game took until 03.30 to finish. At the finish I had been on a phone for over 7 hours and began to appreciate the stamina, concentration (and hearing) required to take part in World Tournaments.

The next night we got lucky and played another British program. This program, written by Bob Prinz, was relatively new to the game and 'blew up' in the opening moves—it thought it had such a strong position that its evaluation function overflowed and it started to look for the worst moves it could play. There was also the idiotic irony of the two programs playing each other via long, expensive links to and from Stockholm when physically the machines were less than 50 miles apart.

In the third round we were lucky again and played a Swiss program, TELL. This program was also underdeveloped and the game was later analysed by a good player, David Pritchard, in the magazine *Games and Puzzles*. It is interesting to see just how good MASTER appeared to be at this point in its career—the point at which MASTER had played about 6 *hours* competitive chess. It is also interesting to read the chess experts' opinions as to why the programs chose their moves.

ROUND 3. MASTER (white) vs. TELL—
ANALYSED BY DAVID PRITCHARD

1	P–K4	P–K4
2	N–KB3	N–QB3
3	B–B4	B–B4
4	P–B3	P–Q3
5	P–Q4	P×P
6	P×P	B–N5+
7	K–B1!	P–KR4

One can almost hear the computer reason "the king is on the king's side and cannot castle so I must attack".

	8	Q–N3!	B–N5
	9	B×P+	K–B1
	10	B×N	R×B
	11	Q–Q5	

A mistake. P–Q5 here wins a piece—but then computers are only human. . . .

	11	...	B×N
	12	P×B	R–R1
	13	N–B3	B×N
	14	P×B	P–R4

Has TELL been told about moving rook's pawns?

	15	QR–N1	Q–B1
	16	B–B4	Q–R6+

Clearly Switzerland, too, knows the old adage 'never miss a check . . .'.

17   K–K2   N–Q1 (see Fig. 9)

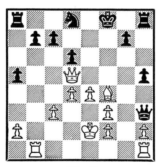

Fig. 9

18   B×P+

It would be interesting to know how far ahead MASTER had been calculating at this point. The sacrifice is certainly sound.

	18	...	P×B
	19	Q×P+	K–B2
	20	KR–N1	KR–N1

White was threatening 21   Q–B7+ to win the KNP.

21   QR–N5

Preparing R–B5+ when White would mate or win Black's queen, so . . .

21	. . .	P–KN3
22	Q–B7+	K–K1
23	R–K5+	N–K3

Black could give up here but COMPUTERS NEVER RESIGN.

24	Q×NP	R–Q1
25	R–N3	Q×P
26	R×N+	K–B1
27	Q–K7++	

The game illustrates the very real precocity of chess programs both in talent and speed. For example, how many beginners would play moves 7 and 8? MASTER really seems to know what it is doing but then blunders at move 11.

The reason for this is that MASTER was undervaluing knights and also because of the Black counter play

11	P–Q5	Q–K1/2
12	P×N	Q×P

and Black has command of the centre plus two squares next to White's king—if the KN is lost then mate is threatened. All this was too vague and dangerous for MASTER's limited look ahead (3 moves on each side) and was rejected. The bishop sacrifice at move 18 gives white control of almost all the top left of the board and was so attractive that it actually only took about 1 second to calculate, a very fast move even for a machine.

On the last night, having won two easy games, MASTER again met a tough opponent, RIBBIT from Canada. At one point in this game Peter Kent, who was in Stockholm, told us that if MASTER won then there was a chance that it could play off for the championship but, unfortunately, TECH 2 had been a costly game in sabbatical time and MASTER was set to play very quickly, missed its chances and gave away a piece. The position at move 54 was (Fig. 10) and Peter Kent asked me if MASTER was saying

Fig. 10

it wanted to resign. Actually the program had been bleating this message out for the previous 10 moves which just proves that computers can resign *but* their authors rarely allow them to.

The reason is simple—of course the game is objectively lost but MASTER had played 54 moves in about 17 minutes of machine time and still had plenty of time on its tournament clock. There are two possibilities still open—White might blunder and give stalemate or (if we delayed our forced replies) RIBBIT's machine might crash and we could even win on a time default.

Unfortunately the British do not stoop to such low tactics, and with cries of "It's taking part that counts!" we rushed to our doom. RIBBIT quickly queened its pawn with a check and mated with Q–N7. I still wonder if it could have done it if the BK had been in QN8 to begin with, the urge to queen a pawn might have overridden a stalemate check but (as we shall see later) RIBBIT has what Napoleon asked of his generals, it's a lucky program.

At the end of the tournament, MASTER had won 2, lost 2 and, on our unofficial tie breaker of how fast a program had won or how slowly it had lost, was placed about fifth out of the thirteen contestants. Total machine time used 1 hour 57 minutes 27·3 seconds.

During the tournament we had not been linked directly to Peter Kent in Stockholm but had been relaying our moves algebraically through London where another chess program was also competing in the tournament. This relay had caused us to use a voice code for the moves (ABLE, BAKER, CHARLIE, DOG, EASY, FOX, GEORGE, HOTEL) and, oddly enough, we never sent or received a bad move.

The troubles with this double link were time problems (not that this mattered after the TECH game but it was never very clear if the total double transmission time was counted on our tournament clock). Also we had almost no idea what had been happening in the other games and no chance to modify the program between games. (In one game we had played 10 moves before finding out what we were playing.)

At the end of the tournament almost all we knew was that CHESS 4·0 had been beaten for the first time in its tournament career and that the winner was KAISSA, the solitary entrant from Russia.

About a week later David Slate and Larry Atkin stopped over in England on their way back to America. They had come second and even played KAISSA to a draw in an exhibition game after the tournament proper. With their recollections (and later, those of Peter Kent when he returned) we were able to piece together what had happened in some of the other games plus some of the atmosphere.

The most striking thing about a computer chess tournament really is the atmosphere. It is a noisy circus with the audience free to loudly comment upon, criticise or applaud the moves of the contestants—a freedom which is fully indulged. Apart from this noise there is the clatter of teletypes, the hum of the machines which are there 'in person' and people shouting moves into telephones.

On top of all this noise and confusion the tournament referee, David Levy, was giving an official commentary on the games as they progressed on big display boards. Levy is an International Master who gives a unique performance on such occasions, he has a tendency to ask the author of a program why it has just played a move—usually a bad move. The author often squirms, mumbles and David Levy then announces loudly over the public address system: "THE AUTHOR SAYS HE DOESN'T KNOW WHY HIS PROGRAM PLAYED THAT MOVE." All good stuff but computers, like elephants, never forget and perhaps one of these days (a wishful thought) a program is going to ask Levy the same question.

The real sensation of the tournament was CHESS 4·0's first loss to another program. This happened on the second night when its opponent was CHAOS, another American entry. The following position was reached after 15 moves (Fig. 11).

CHAOS played 16 N×P!!—a move which has been acclaimed as the "finest ever made by a computer. White evaluates that his domination of

CHESS 4·0

CHAOS

Fig. 11

open lines is compensation for a piece. This judgement is absolutely correct." Of course the piece is not sacrificed entirely and play continues in a very similar fashion to MASTER's sacrifice of a bishop to TELL.

| 16 | ... | P×N |
| 17 | Q×P+ | B–K2 |

CHAOS then developed quickly and put on the pressure

18	R–K1	Q–Q1
19	B–KB4	K–B1
20	QR–Q1	R–R2

and, although CHESS 4.0 was defending well, CHAOS had a grip on the game which it never lost.

The ending was an anticlimax. At move 52 the position was (Fig. 12)

Fig. 12

a won game but CHAOS displayed a typical weakness of chess programs by taking another 27 moves to effect the mate (it can be done in only nine moves: R–K5 then WK×P and queen the rook pawn). This slow win was later to cost CHAOS the chance of a playoff for second place.

At the end of the game, David Levy asked one of the CHAOS authors why it had played the knight sacrifice only to receive the usual reply. However, the author was then heard to mumble that he'd "make damn sure that it never does it again".

Apart from the game there were other, more mechanical problems. Two incidents that occurred in round 3 were particularly amusing. The first again concerned CHESS 4.0 who was playing OSTRICH, yet another American program, which derives its name from the horizon effect. OSTRICH runs on a dedicated Nova computer which is so small and mobile that it was wheeled into the tournament hall and is driven with a demountable disc pack. At move 31 the Nova teleprinter began to give trouble and Monty Newborn, the author of OSTRICH, decided to remove the disc pack, get on a motor bike and try to find another Nova computer. Slate waited patiently in the tournament hall conjuring up visions of Newborn roaring round Scandinavia trying to catch another Nova computer and perform a mind graft in order to continue the game.

Contestants are allowed 20 minutes in the event of machine failure so OSTRICH was only in slight trouble when Newborn eventually stuck OSTRICH's head into another Nova and was able to continue over a telephone link. Despite all these heroics OSTRICH lost on the 48th move.*

Meanwhile a second incident had taken place between KAISSA, the Russian program named after the goddess of chess, and CHAOS. The Americans had input a Russian rook move incorrectly at move 27 (a common *human* error when rooks are sharing ranks or files) and the result had been an apparent mate in two for KAISSA. The telephone link to Moscow had rung off before the CHAOS team discovered their error and appealed to David Levy to restart the game. Efforts to contact Moscow were unsuccessful—probably the Russians were too busy celebrating with vodka—so the audience was treated to yet another new spectacle; the sight of two humans trying to play chess like a computer.

---

* Machines that can balance poles on moving carts and, possibly, ride motor bikes have been developed by Professor Donald Michie.

The two humans were David Levy and Dr. Mikhail Donskoy, one of KAISSA's authors. The situation was doubly ironic for Levy because he is a master chess player who has bet that no program will beat him before 31 August 1978.

Eventually Levy and Donskoy came up with an 11-move continuation which gave a win for KAISSA. This win would become official unless Moscow could be contacted early the next afternoon and continue the game before the final round.

At 5 o'clock the next day the Russians phoned in to find out which program they were to play in the final round. When told the circumstances they sportingly agreed to restart the game and were delighted to see KAISSA find a 9-move continuation to mate, i.e. 2 moves better than the human simulators. Unfortunately nobody asked Levy why he had chosen his moves.

At the end of the tournament Donskoy was presented with a gold medal donated by the well-known publisher Mr. Robert Maxwell. KAISSA had won and the contestants, particularly the Americans, began to analyse its performance.

Probably the best analysis so far is by Dr. Hans Berliner:

> The most intriguing question from the whole event is "what is the structure of KAISSA?" We note that in all its games it had at one point or another a very bad position. Frequently, it blundered right after leaving its opening book. Despite these errors, KAISSA managed to overcome its disadvantages. This appears to be due to the more error-free nature of its subsequent play. Nevertheless, this raises the question as to why it should make errors in what most programmers would consider simple positions.

Berliner chose the most outstanding error as move 8 in the post tournament game against CHESS 4.0.

	CHESS 4.0	KAISSA
1	P–K4	P–Q4
2	P×P	N–KB3
3	P–Q4	N×P
4	N–KB3	P–KN3
5	B–K2	B–N2
6	0–0	0–0
7	R–K1	B–B4
8	N–R4	...

So far KAISSA had played from its book but now it had to compute a move and came up with

8 ...   P–K4

A move which, in Berliner's opinion, gave a significant advantage to CHESS 4.0; also a move which "no self-respecting class 'B' player (1600–1800) would admit having made (if he made it and was shown the analysis, he would claim to have been sick, etc.)".

CHESS 4·0 likes to mess up its opponent's pawns so it took full advantage of the error

9	N×B	P×N
10	P×P	N–N5
11	Q×Q?	R×Q
12	B–KN5	R–Q2
13	N–R3	B×P
14	P–QB3	N/5–B3
15	N–B4	P–QR4?
16	B–B3	P–B3
17	B–R6	P–R5
18	QR–Q1	R×R
19	R×R	K–R1?

At this point Berliner stated that the game was 'essentially won' for CHESS 4.0, i.e. it should win nine times out of ten from the position.

20	B×N	N×B
21	P–B4	P–N4
22	P×B	P×N
23	P×P	R–Q1

If KAISSA's opponent were a class 'B' human then this would be a hopeless end game. Unfortunately for CHESS 4.0 the Russian program noticeably tightened its play from this point and a draw was finally agreed at move 65. A disappointment for Slate and Atkin but even worse was to come.

The fifth United States Championship took place a few months later and was won by RIBBIT; included among RIBBIT's perfect four-point triumph was a victory over CHESS 4.0, their third encounter and third time lucky.

Now the reader should recall that MASTER had lost two games in the World Championship—one to RIBBIT and the other to TECH 2. We were therefore particularly interested to read that the following position had been reached in the third round game between MASTER's victors (Fig. 13).

RIBBIT

TECH 2·0

Fig. 13

It was TECH to play its 23rd move and, in its usual plodding way, it had just sat there and eventually time faulted—how lucky can you get? (The closest equivalent in human play was probably Reshevsky missing a mate-in-two in a world championship qualifying round.)

And so by the end of 1974 it was becoming clear to more and more people that the best chess programs were still capable of the most pathetic blunders. Suggestions, comments and criticisms began to appear from people outside the field of computer chess programs. Many of these people stated that all the World Championship and the fifth ACM tournament had shown was that the brute-force 'crunchers' still didn't know what they were doing—what the programs needed was less searching through massive trees and more of that intangible asset—KNOWLEDGE, the phlogiston of the Artificial Intelligentsia.

CHAPTER 7

The Knowledge Game

FIFTEEN miles east of Palma on the island of Majorca is Mount Randa, a huge saddle-shaped mountain which rises abruptly from the surrounding countryside.

Just below the summit is a cave in which a Spaniard, Ramon Lull, first conceived the idea of machines (*ars magna*) which would be capable of analysing all human knowledge. He called his method the 'art of finding truth' (*ars inveniendi veritatis*) and actually built some machines to demonstrate the method. He was the first person to attempt to build a dispassionate machine.

The most complicated machine, the *figura universalis*, had fourteen concentric wheels and was capable of searching through a staggering number of possibilities in almost every topic of human knowledge. One very practical use of simpler *ars magna* was a method for producing new topics for sermons; a method which Lull described in a book together with 100 sample sermons produced by the machine.

Unfortunately for Lull his work is not well known or treated seriously nowadays; this despite the fact that a monastery to preserve his work and his machines now stands on the summit of Mount Randa and a statue of him was erected in Palma City in 1967.

The problem is partly the suspicion that many people have for Machine Intelligence. The subject is also particularly vulnerable to satire of which probably the most famous example occurs in *Gullivers Travels* by Jonathan Swift.

> We crossed a walk to the other part of the Academy, where, as I have already said, the projectors in speculative learning resided.
>
> The first professor I saw was in a very large room with forty pupils about him. After salutation, observing me to look earnestly upon a frame, which took up the greatest part of both the length and breadth of the room, he said perhaps I might wonder to see him employed in a project for improving speculative knowledge by practical and mechanical operations. But the world would soon be

66

sensible of its usefulness, and he flattered himself that a more noble exalted thought never sprang in any other man's head. Everyone knew how laborious the usual method is of attaining to arts and sciences; whereas by his contrivance, the most ignorant person at a reasonable charge, and with a little bodily labour may write books in philosophy, poetry, politics, law, mathematics and theology, without the least assistance from genius or study. He then led me to the frame, about the sides whereof all his pupils stood in ranks. It was twenty foot square, placed in the middle of the room. The superficies was composed of several bits of wood, about the bigness of a die, but some larger than others. They were all linked together by slender wires. These bits of wood were covered on every square with papers pasted on them, and on these papers were written all the words of their language in their several moods, tenses and declensions, but without any order. The professor then desired me to observe, for he was going to set his engine at work. The pupils at his command took each of them hold of an iron handle, whereof there were forty fixed round the edges of the frame, and giving them a sudden turn, the whole disposition of the words was entirely changed. He then commanded six and thirty of the lads to read the several lines softly as they appeared upon the frame; and where they found three or four words together that might make part of a sentence, they dictated to the four remaining boys who were scribes. This work was repeated three or four times, and at every turn the engine was so contrived, that the words shifted into new places, as the square bits of wood moved upside down.

Six hours a day the young students were employed in this labour, and the professor showed me several volumes in large folio already collected of broken sentences, which he intended to piece together, and out of those rich materials to give the world a complete body of all arts and sciences; which however might be still improved, and much expedited, if the public would raise a fund for making and employing five hundred such frames in Lagado, and oblige the managers to contribute in common their several collections.

The similarities between the Lullian machine described by Swift and a modern computer are strikingly prophetic, particularly the bits linked together by slender wires and the vast amount of useless output. Note also how a lack of funds is the big obstacle. *Tout ca change.*

But to return to more recent times. As we have seen, by the end of the 1950s there was a general air of pessimism by pioneers in the subject to which only Professor Herbert Simon of the Carnegie Institute was an exception.

In the early 1960s new ideas were sought and one of the most interesting directions in this quest was to see whether a computer could be programmed to learn to solve problems; this being one of the most obvious weaknesses of chess programs even nowadays.

This account of some early experiments, reported in 1961 from Bell Laboratories, started from the observation that animals, when set a mechanical problem, usually make purely random actions to begin with (so did Barricelli's symbio-organisms), and then often find the solution by accident. This random activity seemed to be fundamental to acquiring knowledge and it was argued that the reason machines did not learn very well was because they were not sufficiently random.

To overcome this problem Dr. R. Morgan proposed the design of a new type of machine, the CHAOSTRON. The machine was designed from 14,000 Western Electric wiring charts which had been cut into 2-inch (5-cm) squares, thoroughly shaken up in a large sack and then glued into sheets of appropriate size by a blindfolded worker. Careful checks were made during the entire process to ensure randomness and statistical tests were run to make sure that no unsuspected regularities could occur.

Unfortunately this machine was never built but an attempt was made to simulate it in an IBM Stretch computer (so called because it stretched the technology at the time). The simulation language, YAWN, was chosen because it contained at least as much ambiguity as a natural language hence there was no chance that the machine might get an accidental clue as to what it was supposed to do.

Unfortunately this simulation was not possible either and so the experiment was eventually done by simulating Stretch simulating CHAOSTRON on an IBM 704. The problem for the machine was that it would be given a sequence of circles, squares or crosses (these patterns were punched on to cards) and was required to print, after examining each card, the word 'circle', 'square' or 'cross'.

After 133 runs the machine had only made three responses—one of them was to eject the line printer paper twice. Usually the machine ran for an hour or so with no response and the authors concluded that its rate of learning under these conditions was very low—approximately 10^{-6} concepts per megayear.

At this point, despite this promising start, the project encountered budget difficulties (in fact the last 133 runs had been made after the funds had run out) and it was unfortunately abandoned.

So the prospects for a program to learn by itself how to play chess seemed extremely expensive and therefore bleak. However there was another possibility, in fact a possibility much more similar to how humans really improve their own game—why not give the machine some chess books to read?

The first (indeed only) attempt along these lines was made by Barbara J. Huberman and is described by her in *A Program to Play Chess End Games*, published in 1968.

Strictly speaking Huberman's research was concerned with the process of translating a problem solution written for humans into a form that could be used by a computer. The three simple end-game problems chosen for translation were the White king and (rook), (2 bishops), (knight and bishop) versus the Black king. Most chess books would devote about one page to each of these problems; in Huberman's thesis of 168 pages the K, R occupies 16 pages of explanation, the K, 2B occupies 34 pages and the K, B, N occupies 52 pages.

Consider part of Capablanca's explanation (for human consumption) of the K, B, N ending. Given that we have managed to reach the following position (Fig. 14).

Fig. 14

"The second and last part will consist in driving the Black king from QR8 to QR1 in order to mate him (* means forced move)."

10	N–N6+	K–R2*
11	B–B7	K–R3*
12	B–N8	K–R4*
13	N–Q5	K–R5 2

Black tries to make for KR8 with his king. White has two ways to prevent that ". . . the following is more methodical and more in accord with the spirit of all these endings, by using the king as much as possible:

14	K–B5	K–N6 3
15	N–N4	K–B6 4
16	B–B4	K–N6 2
17	B–K5	K–R5 2
18	K–B4	K–R4 2

19	B–B7+	K–R5	* (cf. move 13).
20	N–Q3	K–R6	*
21	B–N6	K–R5	2
22	N–N2+	K–R6	*
23	K–B3	K–R7	*
24	K–B2	K–R6	2
25	B–B5+	K–R7	*
26	N–Q3	K–R8	*
27	B–N4	K–R7	*
28	N–B1+	K–R8	*
29	B–B3++		

"It will be seen that the ending is rather laborious. There are two out-standing features: the close following of the King and the control of the black squares by the bishop and white squares by the knight."

Now the above is usually quite sufficient explanation for an intelligent human to learn how to play the ending. Capablanca assumed that the knowledgeable reader would fill in the details when the BK's move is not forced.

Now this filling in of detail is by no means trivial. Capablanca's explana-tion might be 'sufficient' for a human, but is quite inadequate for a com-puter—a vast amount of additional information must be given to the machine.

For example, the machine must be explicitly warned about creating positions where the N and B are too close to the BK and too far from the WK. One such situation is (Fig. 15)

Fig. 15

in which, if BK–Q4, then white will lose a piece.

In order to guard against producing such situations Huberman's program used the following test (qb = queen's bishop, d = distance) [if $d(kt,qb) \leqslant 2$ and $d(bk,qb) \leqslant 2$ and $d(bk,kt) \leqslant 2$ then white could lose a piece].

Huberman's program used this, and similar tests, to work out its moves. The above is one of the simplest and more understandable, however: "Sometimes it will be necessary to move the knight before the king move can be made. This knight move is a tempo move; it must satisfy kt move

$(p,q) = \{kt_p = kt_q v \ [d_q(wk,bk) = 2 \ \wedge$

$(s(p) > 4 \ \wedge$ location $(p,kt_q,ar(s(p))) = -1$

$\wedge \ d(kt_q,c(ar(s(p)))) = s(p)-2) \ v$

$(s(p) = 4 \wedge$ location $(p,kr_q,ar(s(p))) = 0$

v[location $(p,kt_q,ar(s(p))) = -3 \ \wedge$

$d(kt_q,c(ar(s(p)))) = 4])]\}$"

is an example of the more complicated tests made by the program.

Professor Donald Michie has said that the highest level of machine intelligence "is a 'knowledge machine' able to find out how to do things by reading books". Conversely we might say that the highest level of human intelligence is a person able to find out how to do things by reading a computer program which actually does them.

Personally I am not too fond of Huberman's approach, it exposes the weakness and hides the strength of a computer. The title of the paper is "A Program to Play Chess End Games" and the first impression one gets is that end games must be horribly difficult to program. This is not so: a program which can search ahead only 2 plies almost entirely ensures that it will not lose a piece in any of these three simple endings, thus removing a great deal of Huberman's mind-boggling tests. Apart from this it is quite sufficient (for the R and B, B endings) to only give an incentive to bring the kings together and then search for moves which constrict the BK, to perform the mate. In the case of the B, N ending the program has to also be told which corner to drive the BK into but this is not difficult either.

The tree-searching approach plus minimal knowledge is, however, criticised by the School of Knowledge as being insufficient and inefficient. The tree-search programs do not play perfectly and can take up to 10 moves more than they really need for Huberman's three examples (although they always finish within the 50-move limit). However, it does seem obvious that a simple program which, in a total of 10 seconds machine time, can give mate inside the 50-move rule is more efficient than a complicated program which plays each end game perfectly (with specialised rules) and can take 10 minutes machine time. Unfortunately it is difficult to make genuine comparison because the Knowledge School rarely write a working program.

In actual fact Huberman's program was not a 'perfect player', it used the 'killer heuristic' which "introduces playing inefficiency but is used because the time saved is more important". It is a pity that this first mention of the 'killer heuristic' was so buried in a mass of daunting mathematical notation because it is one of the more useful tricks in the modern computer chess programmers repertoire.

It would be unfair to dismiss Huberman's work as making a mountain out of a molehill. The fact is that a player (human or machine) can often get away with second-rate moves in the middle game but most end games are much more sensitive as to the choice of move. It is not just a matter of the 50-move rule; often the choice of move can be the difference between winning and losing.

The fact that the best chess programs were 'strong amateurs' in the opening and middle game (about class B) and often quite pathetic in the end game had indeed been clearly demonstrated in the 1974 World Championship. In the case of MASTER we were quite aware that it was usually unable to win if it got to Q,K vs K situation but this was a problem which had had to be shelved temporarily in order to concentrate on its opening and middle game—after all what is the point of a program which can win end games if it never gets to a won end game?

After MASTER's 2-hour sabbatical in an IBM 360/195 for the World Championship it was difficult to make a case for any more machine time. The program, yet again, went into an hiatus relieved only by a demonstration against the Hampstead Chess Club on 31 August 1974.

At this point in time MASTER not only lacked knowledge for end games but was also extremely vulnerable in the openings. One of the Hampstead players, Thomas Caswell (rating 1825/153), had watched MASTER play (and lose) a few games before it was his turn. Caswell knew that he could beat the program by merely repeating the moves of any previous game the program had lost—an important psychological point. He also knew that the program was set (if White) to play GIUOCO PIANO opening, so he decided to entertain both himself and the audience with the Wilkes–Barre trap.

Master   *Caswell*

1	P–K4	P–K4
2	N–KB3	N–QB3
3	B–B4	N–B3

at this point MASTER came out of its book and began calculating 6 plies ahead. It saw it could take the KBP so

4	N–N5	B–B4
5	N×BP	B×P+
6	K×B	...

Most people prefer 6 K–B1 but K×B has been played in MASTER's games and is acceptable.

6	...	N×P+
7	K–K3	

MASTER is determined to have the rook but, according to Caswell, this was a real surprise: "Actually it was this which probably won the game for White because I have never seen a reported game in which White did not retire the K by 7 K–N1. I was therefore from that moment entirely on my own."

7	...	Q–K2
8	N×R	Q–N4+
9	K×N	P–Q4+
10	K×P	

If B×P there is a nasty B Q–B5+ 11 K–Q3 Q–Q5+ 12 K–K2 B–N5+ and the X-ray feature tells MASTER that its Queen is lost so it 'horizons'

10	...	P–K5+

At this point both Caswell and the audience knew he should win, he actually has mate in 4 but missed it.

11	K×P	...

and MASTER, 60 miles away in Oxfordshire, could no longer ignore the inevitable loss of the Queen with the horizon effect and began whining that it wanted to resign, but programs are not allowed to resign, and it was whipped on

11	...	B–B4+
12	K–B3	B–N5+
13	K–B2	B×Q
14	B–B7+	K–B1
15	R×B	N–K4
16	B–N3	N–N5+
17	K–N1	P–KN3

and MASTER had weathered the storm. It had also recovered its confidence and now began to develop

18	P–Q4	Q–R5
19	R–B1+	K–N2
20	P–KR3	N–B3
21	B–B4	R×N
22	B–K5!	...

a beauty, MASTER X-rays through both the knight and the king and ignores the pawn capture; Caswell no longer had control of the game.

22	...	R–B1
23	N–B3	P–B3
24	R–B4	Q–N4
25	N–K4	Q–R4

Caswell intended to get his Queen out of trouble via K7

26	N×N	Q–K7
27	N–K4+	K–R3

and the black rook can be taken for a knight but, even better, is the forced

28	R–R4+	Q–R4
29	R×Q+	K×R
30	R–KB1	R×R+

(note that humans never give up against computers in these enlightened times)

31	K×R	K–R3
32	P–B3	K–R4
33	B–KB4	P–KR3

34 N–B6+ K–R5
35 P–N3+ K×P
36 B–K6+ K–R7

and MASTER claimed the win because of

37 N–N4+ K–R6/8
38 N–B2+ K–R7
39 P–N4++

The most important thing about this game is that Caswell had thoroughly enjoyed himself: "It was my deliberate policy to adopt a critical and dangerous defence as I thought this would be more entertaining both for the spectators and myself although clearly, if one is out for a win against a computer, it is wiser to adopt a careful positional line and wait for the computer to make a weak move as it seems inclined to do at the later stages of the game." In other words, play safe and beat the machine in the end game where it is very weak.

Of course MASTER should have lost this game at move 10 by Black playing B–K3+. Another example of it falling into an opening trap was the 'Blackburne shilling game':

MASTER —

1 P–K4   P–K4
2 N–KB3   N–QB3
3 B–B4   N–Q5?

MASTER can take the KP, so in it goes, boots first

4 N×P   Q–N4

Quite good players can miss what is happening and still play 5 N×BP but Q×NP. MASTER sees this and does its best

5 B×P+   K–K2
6 0–0   Q×N
7 P–KB4

and on the whole, manages to wriggle out of the error with a reasonable development.

While MASTER was in post-Championship mothballs we cleaned up its closet of book openings so that it would no longer fall into many of these opening traps. It is possible to do this without running the program, in fact it is possible to rewrite a whole chess program without ever testing it and for a couple of months this is precisely what happened—in particular feedover was debugged and cleaned up.

All these paper improvements should (so we estimated) allow MASTER to run much faster. It would be able to search ahead 7 plies normally but, if conditions allowed (time or simplicity) the program was now capable of 'changing gear'; to search 9 plies ahead and, under really favourable conditions, it would search 11 plies ahead in the simpler end games.

The problem was how to get machine time to test and de-bug the improvements. World Championships are a good excuse but unfortunately only take place every 3 years—fortunately help appeared in the cheerful form of Professor Donald Michie.

Professor Michie is the head of the Artificial Intelligence Department of Edinburgh and possibly Britain's leading expert on Machine Intelligence. He had been invited to chair the first Computer Chess Conference but, because he could not select the speakers himself, had declined.

Quid pro quo, in November 1974 Professor Michie asked me if I would like to help organise and chair the second Computer Chess Conference at Balliol College, Oxford, and this time it was my turn *not* to choose the speakers. As the proposed speakers included Mikhail Donskoy, one of the authors of KAISSA, and Hans Berliner there was no question of my refusing the offer. It also gave us an excuse and a reason to run MASTER again, for an exhibition at the conference.

Between December 1974 and March 1975 MASTER was able to run on an IBM 360/195 for about 40 minutes on Sunday afternoons providing the machine was fairly idle. It was in this period that Peter Kent and John Birmingham produced a program which could be compared favourably with the best Russian and American programs.

We knew this because the machine was matched against better and better players whose ratings were eventually equal to KAISSA and CHESS 4.0, i.e.— 1750/144. On 9 March MASTER played Martin Duck (rating 1744/143). After 30 moves the position was (Fig. 16)

DUCK

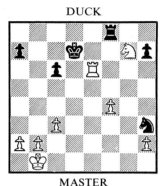

MASTER

Fig. 16

i.e. the program was ahead by two pawns.

It steadily exploited this advantage and, after 49 moves, the position was (Fig. 17)

Fig. 17

which is a clear-cut win for White if it uses the knight as a sacrificial block (N–R4) to gain time to queen first. Of course this was much too far ahead for MASTER to appreciate so the sacrifice was not made. Duck queened first and, muttering something about being late for tea, he left. John Waldron, MASTER's tutor, took over and produced the following position after 73 moves (Fig. 18).

Fig. 18

At this time MASTER, Waldron's *alter ego*, had been taking a beating regularly every Sunday for about 2 months and they were both possibly losing heart. However, the following was really an experiment to see if MASTER could win a simple end game:

74	N–R2	Q–Q4+
75	K–R3	Q×N!
76	K×Q	...

(this took the program 6 milliseconds to calculate)

76	...	K–B4!!
77	P–R7	K–Q5
78	P–R8(Q)	K–K4
79	K–N3	K–Q5
80	Q–B3	K–B4
81	K–B3	K–N4
82	Q–Q5+	K–N3
83	Q–Q6+	K–N4
84	K–Q3?	K–R5
85	Q–B6+	K–N5
86	Q–B4+	K–R4

By then it was obvious that the program had no idea how to win the game. In fact the White king eventually wandered off to K2 and then B2 and the experiment was stopped.

The next Sunday MASTER played as Black against Bob Maybury

(rating also 1744). After Maybury's 26th move the following position was reached (Fig. 19):

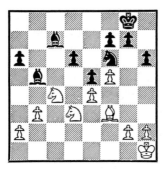

Fig. 19

A happy smile spread over John Waldron's face as MASTER, after 10 seconds calculation, played 26 . . . P–Q4!

Maybury immediately saw the reason for the move and muttered "That pawn ain't going nowhere". Nevertheless he sat and thought for almost 5 minutes before playing on . . .

27	P×P	P–K5
28	B×P	N×B
29	P–QR4	B–Q2
30	P–KN4	P–B3

So for the second time in a week MASTER was, after 30 moves, ahead in a game against a player whose rating equalled that of the best chess programs. Maybury now offered the program a draw by repetition which it refused

31	K–N2	K–B2
32	K–B3	N–N4+
33	K–N2	N–K5
34	K–B3	N–B6

The game continued but, as usual, MASTER eventually blundered in the end game and resigned yet again.

The next week, Sunday, 23 March, was the day before the Chess Conference started and, as a special treat, it was hoped that Bill Hartston, the current British champion, would give MASTER a game. Unfortunately he had a prior appointment but fortunately Dr. Hans Berliner (rating 2376/222) said he would play it.

Most of the conference speakers, including Donald Michie and Ron Atkin, turned up at the Atlas Computer Laboratory to watch this game. All of us knew that the result was inevitable and the main interest was how long the program could last against a really good player like Berliner who also knew how chess programs worked. I later described what happened in a rather flippant article for the *Computer Weekly*:

> Berliner has beaten more chess programs than he has had cold buffets with a good wine. When he arrived at Atlas his dinner and MASTER were waiting for him, and the following are extracts from the log of the game (for M read MASTER, for H read HANS, for O read operator).
>
> M: Right, who's first for a beating?
> O: OK. Hans is Black.
> M: G1 F3; N–KB3.
> O: Hans is eating at the moment.
> M: Surely not food for thought?
> H: Munch, Munch. B8 C6; N–QB3.
> M: Crunch crunch—That's not in my book.
> Silence for 24.3 seconds while MASTER ruminates.
> M: C2 C4; P–QB4 Nodes 24000 value 25.
> H: E7 E5.
> M: (trying to transpose back into book and failing) Crunch Crunch Crunch. . . .
> M: D2 D4; P–Q4 Nodes 57000 value 25.
>   (interval)
> M: Is Hans munching or crunching?
> H: Yes, E5 E4.
> Berliner later went through the game, shown complete in Table 1, explaining some of his early moves. The first one (N–QB3) is standard practice for good players—don't let weaker opponents (particularly machines) play book openings.
> Berliner 'tested' the program twice to try tangling up its development; there were little traps, which he knows programs like CHESS 4.0 (the American program) are liable to fall into. MASTER avoided the traps and developed quite well; in fact by move 11 it had a slight advantage, threatening P–Q5, and Berliner had to play chess for a while rather than continue the interrogation.
> The fact that MASTER lost the game eventually was no surprise to anyone. Berliner has a rating of 222 (British) whereas MASTER only rates about 170 in the opening and middle game. This drops to about 30 for end games which, in this case, it hardly got into. The program's authors were very pleased with its performance against a player of Berliner's calibre.

TABLE 1

			SECONDS	VALUE
1	N–KB3	N–QB3	0	0
2	P–QB4	P–K4	24	25
3	P–Q4	P–K5	57	27
4	N–K5!	Q–B3	24	31
5	N×N	QP×N	22	28
6	N–B3	B–KB4	56	34
7	B–K3	O–O–O	163	60
8	Q–R4	P–QR3	105	88
9	O–O–O	N–R3	65	85
10	P–B3!	Q–K2	58	46
11	Q–R5	P–KN3	17	99
12	Q–K5?	Q×Q	21	90
13	P×Q	R×R+	2	57
14	K×R	B–K3	10	51
15	N×P	N–KB4	45	43
16	B–B4	B×P	40	38
17	P–QN3	B–Q4	41	52
18	N–B6	B–K3	24	63
19	P–K4	N–Q5	47	40
20	B–Q2??	B–QR6!	43	15
21	B–QB4	B×B	38	10
22	P×B	R–Q1	29	29
23	K–K1	P–KR4	74	19
24	K–B2	N×P	50	34
25	B–B1	B×B	38	— 29
26	K×N	R–Q6+	1	— 35
27	K–K2	R–Q7+	7	— 56
28	K–B3	B–N7	22	— 84
29	K–K3	R×P	103	—110
30	K–B4	R–QB7	27	—111
31	R–Q1	R–B6	39	—109
32	K–N5	R×P	26	—100
33	R–Q7	B×P	10	— 97
34	R×P	B×N+	6	— 89
35	K×B	R×P	5	— 95
36	R–B8+	K–Q2	6	—113
37	K×P	R–KR5	105	—121
38	R–B7+	K–Q3	6	— 71

O: A couple of moves and resign . . . OK?
M: Fine by me—this is a difficult one to win.

39	R–B6+	K–Q4	25	—113
40	R–B5+	K–Q5	174	—104
41	R–B2! and resigns.		189	—123

It was quite true that we were pleased with MASTER's performance. Berliner himself had said afterwards that the program was much better than the World Championship version and was now close to the performance of KAISSA and CHESS 4.0. Apart from this Birmingham and

Kent had, in the previous week, given MASTER the minimal knowledge or incentive to bring the kings together in the end game and MASTER had successfully done the K, R and K, B, B endings well within the 50-move limit. It still failed to do the K, B, N ending consistently because it had not, as then, been told which corner to drive the king into.

But all this work impressed the School of Knowledge not one jot at the conference. What was the point (they said) of a program which can get to winning positions against the average tournament player and then, almost invariably, blunder away its advantage in the ensuing end game?

The conference proper lasted 2 days but it quickly became obvious that the audience and speakers were split into three main groups. One group was the Brute Force School; the crunchers who followed the advice of Moltke, a German soldier: "One does what one can, not what one should." A second group was the Knowledge School who openly derided the Brute Force programs as not only inadequate but also a dead end. In the words of Donald Michie, if the cruncher should try his hand at a few endings, "he will discover that the time-honoured methods of enumerating and evaluating hundreds of thousands of look-ahead positions are simply not adequate to plaster over the program's lack of real understanding". The third group in the audience were mainly innocents who found the subject interesting and wanted to know what was going on. For 2 days they were blissfully unaware of the rising antipathy between the pragmatic Crunchers and the prating Knowledgers.

As Chairman I naturally took an unbiased attitude to this escalating feud. Professor Michie's talk was on the K, R vs. K ending and I was intrigued by the fascination this trivial ending seemed to have for the School of Knowledge. Knowing the ratings of many of the people present, I asked six of them the following question, "We have a board which is infinite in the x & y directions thus (Fig. 20).

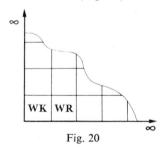

Fig. 20

"The lone Black king is somewhere out there on the board, can he be mated? (Forget the 50-move rule.)"

Five people, with ratings of 1800 or better, said no; the two kings must be brought together to effect the mate and this is impossible. The sixth person already knew the answer. I was impressed by the speed at which humans could answer this problem (about 5 seconds); they saw immediately the hopelessness of the case whereas MASTER with its lack of 'chess knowledge' would be quite incapable of giving any answer at all. Unfortunately the five knowledgeable humans had given the wrong answer.

In actual fact there are a number of chess problems which can be solved very quickly by 'crunch' programs and yet give considerable difficulty to humans. I should point out that one of the standard techniques used by the Knowledge School to belittle the Brute Force School is to set a problem which they know the tree-searching programs, with limited look ahead, cannot hope to solve. (N.B. as I said before it is more difficult to set problems to the Knowledge School's programs as they usually do not exist.) For example, consider the following test (Fig. 21).

Fig. 21

White cannot move his king away from the second rank because of a rook check followed by P–N8 = Q; and for the same reason the White rook dare not leave the QN file except to check.

On the other hand, the Black king cannot support his QN pawn or attack White's NP without being checked on the files or ranks. You are asked to adjudicate the position. What is the verdict?

Every chess program in existence would (effectively) say the position was drawn but human chess players have one great advantage—they make the assumption that BECAUSE THE QUESTION IS ASKED then one side (most probably Black) can win. From this assumption, which has nothing to do with chess knowledge *per se*, they can then perform the correct analysis. The answer is given later.

So the main reason that chess programs often cannot solve an end game problem is because they are NOT TOLD THAT THEY CAN WIN. Given this non-chess specific information they can often solve problems which have baffled many humans.

For example consider the famous SAVEEDRA position, a deceptively simple position which was nevertheless argued over for many years at the turn of the century (Fig. 22).

Fig. 22

Assume a program is playing white and told NOT TO LOSE THE PAWN (i.e. it is equivalent to a king) NOR ACCEPT DRAW BY REPE-TITION. With this information the program easily produces the solution and, if it is capable of under-promotion, eventually wins the game. The answer is given later.

A few weeks after my report of the Balliol Computer Chess Conference had appeared in *Computer Weekly*, I was taken to task by Professor Michie for not giving sufficient emphasis to the importance of machine representations of knowledge. As usual Professor Michie enclosed a position which would stump MASTER plus 99 per cent of the human race (Fig. 23).

"This is an end-game study (from A. A. Troitsky) in which White can win by promoting his pawn. But the promotion strategy alone occupies no

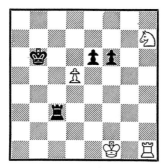

Fig. 23

less than 40 ply of elaborate manoeuvre. . . . What hope would MASTER, or Son of MASTER endowed with the hoped-for 15-ply lookahead, have of finding the winning line?" Now MASTER is a growing lad and wanted to play N×P but this loses the all-important pawn with only a K, R fork as consolation.

As in the Saveedra problem, all MASTER needs to know is the *non-chess Knowledge* that White must promote the pawn to win. We accordingly set the pawn high in value (=K say) and out comes the correct first move P×P (or is it?).

So the great debate at the moment is not whether chess programs need more knowledge in the end game (both the Brute Force and the Knowledge Schools accept this necessity), but about precisely what and how much knowledge is required. My own philosophy is that some chess knowledge is necessary but it should be kept to an absolute minimum, if not then all that results is a program that can play chess and nothing but chess.

Because of my flippancy in the 'cheerfully misleading' article, Professor Michie prescribed for me a penance—that I "should now write a program to play optimal King+Rook vs. King, using no more than 20K bytes of store and no more than 7 seconds for move-retrieval. This exercise is specially designed for converting demon programmers into angels of Artificial Intelligence!"

Although preferring to remain a demon programmer I was resigned to performing this penance. The reason for this was that Professor Michie intended to publish his critique of my miserably misleading attitude. Fortunately the following letter appeared from my old Spanish friend Don Miguel Toros y Gallino:

May 14 1975

Departamento de Intelligenta Artificial
Institute de LULL
SIERRA RANDA
Majorca, Spain.

Querido Alex,

Re: the article on Computer Chess (April 10). This institute has studied end games for many years and I enclose some of our findings.

There are 462 ways of placing 2 kings on a chess board. Of these 378 allow a rook to take one of 48 different positions, 24 allow the rook 49 choices, 20 allow 50, 16 allow 51, 12 allow 52, 8 allow 53 and 4 allow 54.

Therefore there are 22,400 ways of legally placing wk, wr vs. bk with white to play. Of these 189 are mate in one and only one is mate in 17 moves.

We have generated all these positions and then linklisted them into a data base. A program (called COJONES) accesses this structure to recognise any given start position. It then outputs the correct move and how many moves (assuming black plays perfectly) are required to mate.

For example—a forcing sequence is retrieved if the position is WK in c3, WR in c4, and BK in cl.

R–d4 mate in 3
R–d1+ mate in 2
R–c1 mate in 1
R–a1++

If black does not play optimally then the data base is re-accessed for the shorter mating sequence.

The program is called COJONES because the design is based on the work of Prof. R. V. Jones and Dr. C. Bosch concerning the techniques for detecting submarines in the last war. The current search strategy of the data base closely resembles the 'satisfycing search' developed by Professor Herbert Simon at Carnegie-Mellon in America, a technique Simon has applied to finding semi-sharp needles in random haystacks.

Su amigo,
Don Miguel TOROS Y GALLINO.

Of course there was little point in my doing a penance which reproduced this erudite work of the Lullian Institute. I sent the letter on to the *Computer Weekly* and it was published, together with Michie's article, under the title "The Knowledge Game". I excused myself from the penance by observing that COJONES appeared to be the last word on the subject of K, R vs. K ending.

CHAPTER 8

The State of the Art

IN August 1968 MACHACK was demonstrated at IFIPS in Edinburgh. This program was probably the first to have a good chance of beating the casual amateur (rating = 1500/115) and attracted large crowds whenever it played. One of its games during the exhibition was against the chess program written by John Scott, then a 17-year-old schoolboy (see also Chapter 6). Scott's program was the best in Britain at the time but was defeated after a long struggle.

The following week the fourth Machine Intelligence Workshop met, also in Edinburgh. These annual workshops, organised by Professor Donald Michie, not only gathered and published some of the best work in Machine Intelligence from all over the world but were also very enjoyable meetings.

On this occasion, thanks to MACHACK and Scott, the subject and future of computer chess was keenly discussed. Mr. David Levy, who was then the Scottish Chess Champion with a rating of approximately 2250/206, was not impressed by MACHACK and offered a bet that no computer program would beat him at chess across the board for the next 10 years. The bet was accepted by Professor Michie at £250, even odds. Michie was later joined by Professor John McCarthy, Professor Seymour Papert (1970) and Professor Ed. Kozdrowicki (1971),* each of the new members of the consortium staking £250.

Recently Professor Michie increased his wager to £500 and has laid a second wager with Levy (wager accepted) that if Levy loses his bet it will be through defeat by a program developed under Michie's direction. The amount of the second wager is also £500, so Professor Michie has now a total of £1000 at stake and Levy a total of £1750.

The match will consist of two games, one win and one draw is sufficient

* All professors in Artificial Intelligence.

to win the match. What are the chances that Levy will be beaten before 31 August 1978?

With very little time to go the prospect looks remote. Levy now has a rating of 2320/215, yet the best chess programs at the moment are only rated at about 1750/144 and tend to play at a much lower level in the end game. The main obstacle is the expense of developing chess programs. For example, MASTER may have only played 30 hours of chess but the commercial rate for this time on a big machine is about £30,000. Even if Michie does win his bet the charge for machine time (ignoring all development time) would greatly exceed his winnings.

I believe that it is possible with current technology to beat Levy but it would require a massive system of linked computers plus quite gigantic 'knowledge banks' (or databases) and the cost would be astronomical; possibly of the same order of magnitude as the Apollo project. So what can we reasonably expect to happen in August 1978?

The analogy between the Apollo project and developing a chess program can be extended. Dr. Werner von Braun, who developed the brute-force Saturn V stage of Apollo, had this to say after the first successful Moon landing:

> Let me say this, in retrospect, with all the advantage of twenty twenty hindsight, I sometimes wonder at the naïveté that I myself and many of my associates had in the early days. For example the problem of navigating to the Moon and making a pin point landing where you desire looks awfully simple in a motion picture. But when you have to do it . . . it's a very, very difficult problem. I ask myself sometimes how we ever hoped to solve these problems without the help of the fantastic computation machines that we have today.

This statement is an acknowledgement by von Braun that his massive Saturn V solved only the first part of the problem of making a Moon landing. It was in fact (indeed it had to be) computers which controlled and navigated the astronauts to and from the Moon; humans only flew the last 50 feet down to the Moon's surface.

By 1978 we can confidently expect an equivalent to the Saturn V in chess programs and it is my belief that such a brute-force program that could search full width and 15 plies deep, would have a good chance, on purely tactical play, of detecting an error by David Levy and his peers during the middle game. This is partly based on an analysis of some of his games; he has made tactical blunders at only 5 plies. Donald Michie has also said:

> Alex Bell has stated . . . that at 15-ply Levy will crumble. If I may add the qualification 'in the mid-game', then I agree with him. Faced with that degree of

long-range tactical accuracy Levy will be up against something fast and slithery, which once in a while will catch him napping. Before the mid-game is out it is likely that some trap or another will have been sprung, a pawn or two (even a piece) will have been snatched; and the program will enter the end-game in the lead.

"But what is the use", we may ask, "of a program which reaches the end game with a winning advantage, only to commit hara-kiri by playing like a moron?"

Unfortunately, Professor Michie is correct; a 15-ply tactical program will fall apart against Levy in an end game just as the 7-ply MASTER falls apart at the moment against lower-class players. The 15-ply program is, like the Saturn V, a *necessary* but *not sufficient* part.

The possibility of constructing a 15-ply program I leave until the next chapter. For the moment let us assume that we have one, that we can get a slight advantage in the mid-game by sheer tactical play. How can a program realise its advantage?

One possibility is that the program should (some people would say must) begin to simulate, more and more, how the human chess player solves the problem of selecting a move. Now the main thing that distinguishes the master player from the ordinary player (and the computer) is that he has vastly superior *pattern recognition of goals* in chess positions. By this I mean that 'true purpose of the position' is recognised and understood. Adrian de Groot repeated and extended a classic experiment (first performed by the Russians) which clearly distinguished this ability in the strong player.

In this experiment the subject is shown a genuine middle-game position for about 5 seconds. Grandmasters can reproduce such positions on another board with about 95 per cent accuracy, i.e. 95 pieces out of 100 will be replaced correctly. The average club player in such an experiment is found to score well below 50 per cent.

If the chess positions displayed are random—the pieces are placed haphazardly—then performance becomes indistinguishable. Most people can only replace about 15 per cent of the pieces irrespective of their chess skill.

The conclusion drawn from these experiments is that grandmasters do not think faster or deeper but, due to superior pattern recognition, they do think about the right things. A startling example of this phenomena occurred when ex-World Champion, Max Euwe, was interrupted after 10 seconds viewing of a particularly difficult position. Euwe was able to reproduce the position with only two errors insignificant to the play that was to follow. Further, he was able to identify the core problem in the position and had plans formulated for exploration. Most remarkable, he had already intuitively selected the winning move (which three masters, five experts, and a number of average players had failed to do during a complete analysis) and was able to visualise a possible variation.

The recognition and reconstruction of a position is done from short-term memory. G. Miller, in an article "The Magical Number Seven, Plus or Minus Two", proposed a short-term memory model with a capacity of about seven 'chunks'. The master player recognises a meaningful position by mapping it into about seven chunks, i.e. for about twenty-five pieces recalled he must recall about four pieces per chunk. His advantage is that, due to experience, he has amassed an enormous vocabulary; a rough estimate is that he can recognise about 100,000 different clusters of pieces. Here is one of them (also the most likely position these pieces will occupy at the 21st move in a master chess game) (Fig. 24).

Fig. 24

This is a familiar pattern to most good chess players. Experiments on eye movements have shown that master players hardly look at any of these pieces, their peripheral vision informs them of a pattern which they have seen thousands of times; the properties and purpose of this 'superpiece' are well known and the pieces are not, nor need to be, distinguished individually.

Unfortunately, although the seven patterns or chunks do explain how master players can reconstruct positions, it is not at all clear how these patterns suggest strong, plausible moves and so trying to simulate the exact methods of a strong player—methods derived from many years of experience staring at chess positions in games between experts—is not a very promising line of approach to a World Champion Chess Machine at the moment. Until more understanding is obtained we must do what we can, not (in all likelihood) what we should.

However, one approach, developed by Zobrist and Carlson at the University of California, is indeed the identification and selection of moves for consideration in the game tree based upon the move fulfilling a 'pattern of interest' to a very good player, in this case Charles Kalme who has a rating of 2445/230. This idea of Kalme teaching a program the important 'chunks' of chess positions is an extremely attractive one and of great psychological interest but the program *still* looks for the ten best moves at each position and builds the traditional, ponderous trees for mini-maxing, primarily because the patterns are almost entirely keyed to single moves (rather than combinations or sequences of moves) and involve only very simple relationships between two pieces or a piece and a square (rather than involving more complex groupings of pieces).

Now, as I have already said, the really important difference between a human player and a machine is that the machine looks hopefully out into the future whereas the good human player sees a plan or a goal. He often sees that getting a piece to a certain square will give him an advantage and he then works backwards, from the goal position to the present position, to see if his plan is feasible. A program along these lines, i.e. one that identifies an objective at the end of a path before generating any moves to determine whether the path can be realised, is being developed under the direction of Mikhail Botvinnik who (Reshevsky, again please note) was World Chess Champion from 1948 to 1963.

This idea is again attractive in that it attempts to truly simulate the human method—the creation of a plan of attack—but it has been 6 years since Botvinnik's book, full of glowing optimism, was published and the project has perhaps run into trouble.

The reasons are not hard to guess. One reason is that Botvinnik is not a programmer and, although his method is highly mathematical, he seems to have an incomplete appreciation of the art of computing, an art which depends on simplicity not complexity. Another reason is that his program will not select as few goals as a human player and therefore must spend a lot of time tree searching albeit in reverse. But is tree searching the only approach?

In fact a mathematical, non-tree-searching approach has been suggested in an analytical system proposed by Ron Atkin and Ian Witten. The word 'ply' is anathema to Atkin and the approach is extremely abstract, to the point of being almost impossible to visualise or explain except through mathematical symbology.

Each position is described in terms of a vector space in 53-dimensional Euclidean space and uses mathematical concepts of simplices and connectivity between them to provide quantitative values representing piece co-operation, mobility, and tactical flexibility. The program has not been designed to play complete games but, by maximising the above listed values, it has produced move decisions that compare 'reasonably well' with those made by grandmasters in well-known games. The method quite obviously has no relationship with human chess thinking and is also quite unable to appreciate tactical situations like captures, checks or even checkmate.

With the help of Bill Hartston, the current British champion, the program has been developed into a three-level structure; very roughly the first level deals with tactical play and the higher levels deal with positional play. Hartston has asserted "that it annotates better than Golombek".

Atkin and Kepler are two of my favourite mathematicians because both of them are (were) fascinated by description. In Kepler's case he succeeded in showing that the five Platonic solids could be used to describe the distances of the six planets (Mercury, Venus, Earth, Mars, Jupiter, Saturn) from the Sun. Unfortunately Kepler's description (although it fitted all the then known facts) fell into disrepute when the planet Uranus was discovered.

Now it is quite true that any chess position can be described in 53-dimensional space but such descriptions are frequently sterile. Science is concerned with prediction which is why both Kepler's and Atkin's models are not very helpful, they might describe but they do not explain and therefore cannot suggest how to continue further investigation of either the solar system or a chess position.

Nevertheless Atkin's program does not search trees and, despite its tactical failings, it can give very detailed positional annotation. At present the brute-force programs definitely falter and fail in non-tactical situations and it could well be that, in such situations, the only way to continue sensibly is to make sound positional moves. In fact it is very likely that a combination of 'brute-force tactics' and 'Atkin positional play' will be a way to overcome David Levy, but this welding of techniques into one program is not an easy task.

The plain fact is that there is no simple way to reach human master level; no trick in maths, programming, knowledge or psychology that can replace the years of hard concentration that David Levy and his colleagues have spent in order to play as well as they do—but is this so wonderful? Most of us can, for example, recognise and name thousands of people and objects; an ability which also far surpasses anything yet achieved by a machine.

As Shannon pointed out, computers do have their strengths and conversely humans have their weaknesses. For example, in 1957 Edward Lasker, the New York chess master, played Arthur Samuel's draughts program. In Lasker's words:

> I play checkers worse than chess, but I felt I could easily see three moves ahead. . . . In the early middle game, out of a clear sky, the computer sacrificed one man, and then two more. I was just about to make a polite remark to Dr. Samuel about the machine's deplorable oversight, when I noticed to my horror that no matter what I played . . . the machine would win back the three men with the better game.

Lasker finally won after a hard battle but admitted that the machine had nearly beaten him.

Another example to make the point. There is a game called Monster Chess which has the following initial position (Fig. 25).

Fig. 25

Black, the monster, is compensated for lack of material by being allowed to make 2 moves for each White move, the Black king can also move through a check square providing he eventually finishes out of check. Apart from this all the rules are as usual—and yet I have seen Bill Hartston beaten in this game by a player who had no chess rating and MASTER would beat David Levy in this game unless he put in a lot of practice.

What these two examples show is that very good chess players are very highly specialised, indeed their knowledge is possibly a handicap when they are faced with any problem outside the very narrow confines of normal chess. A slight change in the rules and the patterns are useless. Such experiments re-emphasise the fact that master players are no better at tree searching than ordinary mortals and very much weaker than machines.

To really rub this in consider the possibility of a pentathlon of board games for the World Championship and let the games be Chess, Draughts, Go, Backgammon and Kalah. I have absolutely no doubt that the winner of this hypothetical event would be a program using five simple evaluation functions coupled, in turn, to a powerful general tree-searching procedure and running in a powerful computer.

In short I am completely satisfied with the performance of computers playing a variety of games against mere humans. They are already more versatile and flexible in many of the activities that we call 'intellectual' in the same sense that the wheel surpasses the human leg. In the final chapter I will completely ignore human simulation, knowledge, psychology, predictions and wishful thinking to concentrate on the programming techniques which are almost completely devoid of knowledge (chess or otherwise) and (apart from more powerful machines) have been and will continue to be the major source of improvement for at least the next 5 years. Beyond that point in time we might find, as von Braun did, that a completely new type of machine will solve the difficulties of the last lap and reveal our current *naïveté*.

CHAPTER 9

Machine Technique

IN A typical chess position the average number of possible moves is about 30. This number drops to about 20 in the end game thus (Fig. 26).

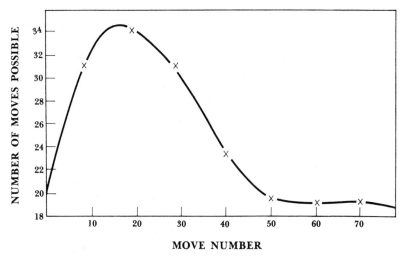

Fig. 26

The typical game lasts about 40 moves. Assume that we (human or machine) can identify ten 'reasonable' possibilities at each move, i.e. about 3 moves by White and 3 replies to each. There are therefore 10^{40} possible games.

Suppose we have a machine that can play a game every nanosecond (= 1,000,000,000 games per second) and we have a million such machines on the job full time. Finally assume that all these super machines have been

95

working since the solar system first appeared ($= 10^{18}$ seconds). The result is that we would have only analysed one ten-millionth of all these possible games.

The above is often used as a fatuous proof that computers will never be able to play perfect chess—fatuous because it is an equally valid proof that humans cannot attain perfection either.

But what if we restrict ourselves to only the first 10 moves? Of course the result after only 10 moves is not going to be as 'obvious' as it would be after 40 moves but there exists a wealth of analysis on the openings and, if this were fed into a data base, the machine could make a taxonomic check (i.e. look for the position closest to the one it has produced after 10 moves) and take the human assessment as to whether White or Black has the advantage or that the game is even.

There is therefore no valid reason why a computer should not play the opening game faster and better than any human living or dead (particularly the latter). So why hasn't it been done?

The main reason is that it is an expensive, time-consuming job for a human to collect and enter all the available information—nevertheless, once it has been done (plus an update facility as new variations appear), it need never be done again. Another advantage would be that humans could interrogate this data base and the machine could regurgitate examples of when and where last played plus the reasons as to why, in the opinion of expert human analysers, certain moves were thought preferable to others. By the end of this century a computer will almost certainly be the best commentator on the opening moves in a World Championship.

Now many chess programs do have a 'book' of openings but they are extremely small in comparison to the above proposal. The purpose is mainly to save machine time (i.e. the machine is quite capable of playing sensible openings with its tree searching) and almost always they cause problems.

One problem with these rather *ad hoc* books is that many openings just do not suit the following style of play of the tree search evaluation. When the book line runs out the machine no longer has a stored response. It then begins to search and often (KAISSA is a good example) finds that the current position is, in its terms, extremely bad. With no information as to the theme or purpose of the opening the machine tries to rebuild what is known to be a sound position into a position which it likes.

So it is important to match the book to the machine's style. A more specific example is MASTER which currently 'digs in' during the book moves, e.g. 1 N–KB3 2 P–KN3 3 B–N2 4 0–0.

On emerging from the book MASTER's evaluation is very keen to control the centre squares. Thanks to the book's reticence it often finds plenty of moves which improve its centre control plus, if the opponent has been more aggressive, plenty of enemy pieces in the centre to attack.

In order to look ahead the machine has to generate lists of moves. This is often described as trivial but it is also crucial—the moves must be produced as fast as possible. Most chess programs use a 10 by 12 board numbered thus (Fig. 27).

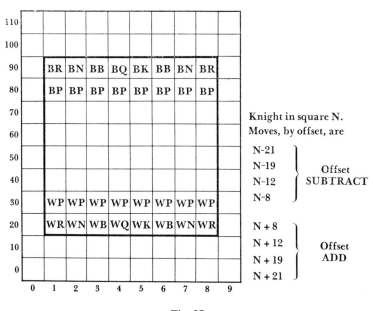

Fig. 27

The border is artificially filled with friendly pieces and its purpose is to detect when pieces (particularly knights) are trying to move off the board. A White knight in QN1 would generate, by offsets, a list of eight possibilities, 1, 3, 10, 14, 30, 34, 41, 43, and have to then reject six of them. The techniques to obtain the moves of other pieces are essentially the same and it is a traditional, trivial and rather inefficient method which immediately demonstrates the difference between a computer and a human—the machine can only deal with essentially YES or NO situations—concepts like large, small, near, far, better, worse are not understood by machines (although, sooner or later, this may be possible).

Using the legal move generator the machine now examines the result (immediate and remote) of making each of the possible moves, the replies thus opened to the opponent, the possible replies to these moves, etc. How a move is chosen was first described in detail by Shannon in his classic paper. He gave the diagram shown in Fig. 28.

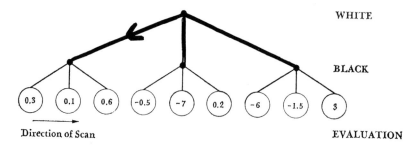

WHITE

BLACK

Direction of Scan   EVALUATION

Fig. 28

"It is assumed that there are three possible moves for White, indicated by the three solid lines, and if any of these is made there are three possible moves for Black, indicated by the thinner lines. The possible positions after a White and Black move are then the nine circles, and the numbers within are the evaluations for these positions. Maximising on White's move, we obtain 0.1 and White's best move is arrowed."

It took 15 years for the superior pattern recognition of humans to realise that it is not necessary to search the whole tree. In Shannon's diagram it is indeed necessary to look at all three evaluations to find the left-hand minimum ($= 0.1$) but the instant the machine picks up the -0.5 in the middle three it need look no further and, similarly, picking up -6 in the last three can also terminate the minimising. This cut off is called the ALPHA–BETA PROCEDURE.

Once this was realised (and even Samuel had missed it in his very strong checkers-playing program), a little mathematical analysis revealed that if the moves were in optimum order the time taken to search the tree could drop to about the square root of its original value, i.e. a program which had taken 100 seconds could, with alpha–beta, produce the same choice of move in about 10 seconds.

Of course, this square-root improvement is never achieved in practice because no one knows how to order the moves optimally (if we did then we would not need to search at all and the improvement is, strictly speaking infinite). Nevertheless even the roughest sort when the moves are generated (for example, checks, captures and then other moves) can produce considerable improvements in cut off and speed of play.

Another trick of the trade is called REFUTATION or the KILLER HEURISTIC. This trick is particularly attractive because it also requires no knowledge (chess or otherwise).

To show the principle consider Prinz's two-move mate problem (discussed in Chapter 4). Alpha–beta is no help at all in such problems because the evaluation is only binary (only one of the opening moves guarantees checkmate, all the rest would just return failure).

Assume that Prinz's program is investigating the correct move (R–R6) and the reply (B–B2). The program now generates 5 possible moves for the White king (2 are illegal), 2 moves for the White pawn and 1 move for the White rook. It investigates these eight moves and finds that R × P + + is the correct move.

At this point the program has to try another Black response so it tries B–Q3. The program now generates 5 possible moves for the White king (3 are illegal), etc. All refutation does it to avoid this repetition by remembering the single move which refuted B–B2 (i.e. R × P + +) and trying it immediately if it is still possible. In this way all the six bishop moves after the first are quickly 'killed off' and it is not until Black plays P × R that another refuting move (P–N7 + +) has to be found.

Although a simple principle, refutation is quite difficult to program and use correctly in a chess-playing program. However, tests have shown that in two-move mate problems a five-fold increase in speed can be obtained on average.

Another simple trick which has often been overlooked is called CHOPPER. What this says is that if all alternatives except one are obviously bad then take the one remaining *without* any further investigation.

The most obvious use of CHOPPER is when a program has only one move, for example the king has to move out of check. This may seem trivial but many programs, including TECH 2 when it played MASTER at

IFIPS, actually spend a few minutes searching through plies 2, 3, 4, etc., before deciding that their best choice is their only choice.

A more subtle use of CHOPPER occurs when a chess program is told that one side or the other can win. Take the SAVEEDRA position, for example (given in the last chapter).

When humans are given this problem they are usually told that White can win (if they are not told anything they quickly suspect this possibility anyway—this suspicion has nothing to do with chess knowledge, but is fundamental to solving many problems). They then argue that if White can win, then the pawn is worth more than the rook—and at this point a program can now solve the problem.

The program looks ahead 4 plies and finds that only one move (P–B7) can save the pawn. So it makes the move without further investigation. Using CHOPPER the problem unfolds—the White king is forced to move down the knight file in order to keep the pawn and also to avoid a draw by repetition. Eventually the White king has to play to QB2 and I leave it to the reader to judge whether R–Q5 (which prevents the pawn from queening because of a stalemate threat) is the best move for Black at this point. A computer usually assumes that its opponent is as intelligent as itself and would expect R–R6.

Another example, which CHOPPER can speed up enormously, is "Can you win with R, KP, KBP, KNP, KRP vs. R, KBP, KNP, KRP?" Well sometimes you can and sometimes you can't. The expert knows that the defender must try to get his RP to KR4; if he can then the game is probably drawn. It is this hard-earned knowledge that is the main advantage of the expert against a computer because, if the machine knows this fact also, it is at least the equal of the expert in getting where it wants to get and, thanks to CHOPPER, vastly superior in speed of play.

There are many other tricks which speed up the generation and searching of chess trees but I will consider only one more. Like many of these techniques it is simple, obvious but difficult to implement into a machine—it is called FEEDOVER.

In a chess program much effort is put into sorting moves into the best order at the various plies. This transforms an initially random tree into an highly ordered structure with alpha–beta values and refutations plus (if applicable) any chops on branches. In the majority of programs a move is then selected and the whole tree is thrown away. At the next move the machine behaves as though it has never seen the position before and laboriously rebuilds the tree. Sometimes as in the case of COKO, it can even miss something it had seen in the previous analysis.

All this seems very wasteful and is prone to error therefore, in the case of MASTER, the most important parts of the tree are saved in order to (1) speed up the searching process on the next move, (2) to hang on to any strong sequences (particularly checkmate), and (3) to aid in debugging by having the program report what it thinks is the most likely continuation of the game, i.e. what it thinks is the opponent's best move and what it then intends to play.

FEEDOVER was designed and written by Peter Kent and John Birmingham in about 2 days but it took many hours of testing to avoid some of the difficulties it raises in implementation. Nevertheless a crude form currently (along with alpha–beta, refutation, chopper and other tree-pruning techniques) allows MASTER to play at 9 plies when it emerges from the opening with the option of changing down to 11 and even 13 plies if time and the position permit.

As MASTER is written in a PL/1, a slow, high-level language, and as new machines are coming on the market which are some 10 times faster than current models, it therefore seems quite feasible that chess programs will reach 15 plies of tactical play in the near future.

At this depth they will indeed give David Levy a hard, tactical game— they may even get to an objectively won game—but they will never beat him because (and this is both their strength and weakness) they still will not know what they are doing.

The main reason they do not know what they are doing is that too much knowledge slows up the deep tree search. Parameters in the sorting and evaluation must be cheap to compute or necessary, i.e. either speed up play, improve the ordering of the moves or correct a fault observed in actual play.

MASTER has some chess knowledge but it is deliberately kept as small as possible and only put in with reluctance. The parameters of this knowledge are:

(a) Material value.

(b) Attacks on pieces by lower valued pieces or on inadequately defended pieces.

(c) Hidden attacks—pins, X-rays, skewers.

(d) Position of pieces (e.g. knights are weak at the edge of boards).

(e) Pawns increase in value (passed pawns very rapidly) as they advance (equal to opponent's lowest piece when they reach the 7th rank).

(f) Control of squares (central squares are highly valued at the beginning but, as the game progresses, this attraction fades and the squares around the opponent's king become more attractive).

(g) Doubling of rooks, queens and bishops.

(h) Attacking passed pawns, the squares in front of passed pawns and blocking passed pawns (see Chapter 7, MASTER vs. DUCK for the reason this knowledge was fed in).

(i) The king is encouraged to go to KN1 in the first part of game and then, after half the material has gone for either side, it will try to move to the centre.

(j) Opposition of kings.

(k) Move kings together when opponent only has a king. With this MASTER can perform the (K and Q, R or 2B) versus K mate at just 3-ply look-ahead. This rule can also help to solve the adjudication problem given in the previous chapter—get the BK to Q6 and a 15-ply look-ahead can easily see how to win the game.

(l) Keep the king next to pawns (again helps to solve the adjudication problem).

(m) Castling.

By now the reader should have some idea of what he would be up against should he ever play a machine. But will this help either you or David Levy to beat a chess program in the next few years? The reason I ask this question is that chess programs are still advancing rapidly in sophistication and when faced 'over the board' have other, more psychological advantages which are only just being exploited.

For example, CHESS 4.0 makes comments on the opponents' moves. If the move is a good one then it might say 'Oh, you did that.' On the other hand, if the opponent plays slowly he is liable to get the message 'Time sure flies' come up on the screen. Some comments are even more sarcastic, and are calculated to amuse the audience and embarrass the opponent.

A phenomenom that is very noticeable with chatty chess programs is that the audience is very interested what the machine 'thinks' about the current position. On one occasion when MASTER was giving an exhibition its opponent positively insisted on having the machine's assessment of the position with every move it made and seemed to derive comfort from the fact that it remained steady and was noticeably relieved whenever the score dropped.

To illustrate one effect of knowing the machine's evaluation I will finish with a game against MASTER.

As usual the program had gone into mothballs after the second chess conference in March 1975. It was resurrected in August as a special treat (I was leaving the country) and actually played a transatlantic game with Richard Cichelli in Pennsylvania. The next week we hoped to retest this historic transatlantic link but no contact was made—so I played it for the last time.

The program itself is actually resident inside the machine at all times but, in order to control its playing speed and evaluation, a number of punched cards are read in to begin with. Also read in is the current opening book.

One now sits down in front of a visual display unit which resembles a television set and has a set of typewriter keys. The program comes up and asks, on the screen, what colour you want.

	BELL (White)	vs.	MASTER (Black)
1	N–KB3		N–KB3
2	P–KN3		P–Q4
3	B–N2		QN–Q2
4	0–0		P–B4
5	P–Q3		...

A surprise here. MASTER did not know this opening and began to compute. To do this it claimed top priority in the machine and all other work in the machine came to a halt. In contrast to the rapidity (almost instantaneous) of the book play, the program takes a very long time to compute its first move (about 5 minutes) because it has to initialise a vast amount of storage and build up the first FEEDOVER. From now on the program displays (and this was to cause me problems) an evaluation of the current position in its terms. (See also Berliner's game in Chapter 7.)

			Value
5	...	P–K3	10
6	B–N5	B–K2	20
7	P–B3	P–KR3	30

			Value
8	B × N	B × B	30
9	Q–R4	0–0	40
10	N–QR3	N–N3	40
11	Q–N5	N–Q2	40
12	Q–R4	N–N3	40
13	Q–N5	N–Q2	40

Up to this point I had been taking advantage of what I knew the program would try to do, i.e. I did not go anywhere near the centre so when it came out of the book it was a little lost. I also knew it would try to push its queen side pawns at about move 10 so, out of curiosity, I had put my queen against them. The program had offered a draw by repetition which I pointed out to Peter Kent and complained that it was up to me to break this deadlock. No sympathy was forthcoming so . . .

14	QR–Q1	P–QR3	40
15	Q–R4	N–N3	60
16	Q–R5	N–Q2	30
17	Q × Q	R × Q	50
18	P–K4	P–QN4	50
19	KR–K1	P–N5	20

The speed (a few seconds) of this move amazed and slightly annoyed me, it was still blindly and pathetically advancing its pawns. Also I was tired of playing quietly and felt like some 'wood pushing'

20	P–K5	P × N	80
21	P × B	RP × P	110
22	P × P	K × P	130
23	N–K5	N × N	140
24	R × N	R–Q3	170
25	P–QB4	B–N2	170

The program at this point thought it was doing well because it had got a pawn to the 7th rank. I intended to disillusion it

26	R–N1	R–N3	140
27	P × P	R–QN1	140
28	P × P	B × B	130

29	K×B	P×P	110
30	R×BP	K–B3	110
31	K–B3	R–N5	140

When MASTER gets a score of 200 or more it usually means that it is genuinely winning. At this point I had brought its score down but it still thought that the advanced pawn was worth a lot. We have now reached an end game in which the superiority of my human knowledge will win the day

32	R–B2	P–QR4	120
33	K–K2	P–R5	130
34	K–Q2	P–R6	140

So it is now three against three (and it still thinks it's doing well, but I know I'm going to beat it to a pulp, after all this is an end game. Kent just sits there).

35	R–B4	R(5)–N4	140
36	R–QR4	R–KB4	110

Horizon effect, it is just delaying the inevitable so, without too much thought,

37	P–B4	R–KR4	130

Horizon effect again, when is it going to face up to its problems like a man?

38	P–R4	R–QB4	60
39	R×P	R(4)–N4	50

His score is coming down nicely now

40	R–N3	R×R	0
41	P×R	R×P	−50
42	K–B2	R–N4	−60
43	R×P	R–QR4	−70

Pow! And let that be a lesson to you. Now for the *coup de grâce*, how could I not win? Well it was tea time and I was in a hurry

44	R–N6	R–R7+	−60
45	R–N2	R×R	−60
46	K×R	K–B4	−40

47	P–Q4	K–N5	−10
48	K–B3	K×P	−0
49	P–B5?	P×P	30

I blew it, it's not just chess programs that play pathetic end games

50	P–Q5	P–B5	10
51	P–Q6	P–B6	50
52	P–Q7	P–B7	10

Draw agreed.

Turing said of his paper machine after its game with Glennie: "If I were to sum up the weakness of (my) system in a few words I would describe it as a caricature of my own play." After my game with MASTER I felt like summing up my play as a caricature of the machine's weaknesses. Peter Kent just grinned.

At the end of a game a massive amount of output is printed by the program in order to check out some of its decisions. In my game it had predicted my next move 23 times and, even more significant, had made its feedover move almost 90 per cent of the time. It had also expected my 49th move to be P–Q5.

So much for a program which has played about 30 hours of chess. I leave it to the reader to imagine what another 970 hours practice might achieve.

Addendum

I PLAYED my last game with MASTER because we failed to re-establish a Transatlantic link with Richard Cichelli on that Sunday. I left England the next week believing that this was a temporary failure and that MASTER would be able to play in the ACM tournament in October; the machine time and the links had been approved and fully tested out, and Cichelli had agreed to represent the program at the tournament.

I received the following letter from Richard Cichelli just 2 days before submitting this manuscript. I trust posterity will appreciate (as David Levy obviously has) that a big obstacle to developing a chess program is any contact whatsoever with officialdom who 'know' that computer chess is just a game.

A. G. Bell
Division of Computing Research
CSIRO
P.O. Box 1800
Canberra City, A.C.T.
Australia 2601

30 November 1975

Dear Alex:

I suspect that Kent's told you that getting MASTER into ACM '75 was a lot more of a problem than originally thought. Col.   , head of   , thinks chess programming is politically unsuitable for the network.

Anyway, I enclose a copy of my last letter to Kent. It includes lots of tourney news. Sorry about MASTER—we tried.

I'll send you a tape of my PASCAL stuff soon as I get over to Lehigh during the day. It is for PASCAL I.

Slate is considering writing a new chess program in PASCAL.

Sincerely,

Richard J. Cichelli

Mr. Peter Kent
Science Research Council
Atlas Computer Laboratory
Chilton—Didcot—Oxfordshire
England

Dear Peter,

Thank you very much for the chess programming literature. Levy is publishing an analysis of the ACM '75 tourney available in February:

ISBN 0–914894–01–3   *1975 U.S. Computer Chess Championship*
Computer Science Press, Inc.
4566 Poe Avenue
Woodland Hills, Ca. 91364
Cost: $3.95 for paperback

As you probably know, Allen Newell and Herbert Simon received the Turing Award this year. They mentioned their chess programming research during their acceptance speeches. It is really amazing the fame that awaits chess programmers, if they just obtain the maturity to stop chess programming!?!

I spoke with Newell about our problems with ****. He was astonished and chagrined. He said, "I'll have to talk to Dave about that." He requests that you send to him copies of the relevant correspondence (at Carnegie-Mellon University, Pittsburgh, Pa., USA). He assures me that he will at least be able to straighten things out for next year. I believe Newell can help everyone concerned. You owe it to yourself to pursue this. ****** deserves to get some heat.

Now for some fun!

This is the story of the little program that almost wasn't there. Because of my plans for tournament participation, we (Martha & I) arrived a day early for the conference. I attended the tourney organisational meeting just to confirm our withdrawal. Newborn said that since I was there would I care to monitor another program. The program was authored by a previous tournament gadfly, Garth Courtois, at the University of Colorado. I had met Garth and owed him a favor from previous years. Anyway, to make a long story short (?), I accepted the duties.

Monty Newborn assured me that the program was a born disaster. Garth was an unemployed chemist and knew very little chess, less computer science, and possibly zip about how to write a chess program. (Insert condescending Newborn smile here.)

Well, Garth certainly had the world stacked against him. His computer was an obsolete Nova mini that was sort of forgotten in a closet in the E.E. building at the University of Colorado. No one even knew he was using it. This old Nova had about half the horsepower of Newborn's spanking new one, and it was smaller. Garth had the most modest hardware of the tourney.

We were seated 10th simply because the 11th and 12th ranked entries were known to be absolutely terrible. And it didn't help that the program's name was unpronouncable . . . ETAOIN SHRDLU . . . named after the first two key columns of the linotype. David Levy baptised it E.S.

Round 1   The luck of the draw. Paired against Monty Newborn's OSTRICH.

"I'm sorry about sticking you with this program, Dick, but it is so bad at least the games won't last long," said Professor Newborn with great consolation in his voice.

I smiled, thinking four letter words.

Well, the opening went better than expected and Newborn finally admitted OSTRICH had bungled the opening. We were in the thick of the middle game, even material, and SHRDLU had all its pieces out on the offensive. OSTRICH sat with a bishop, knight, and rook stuck in a corner.

"It's not playing a bad game so far." Newborn was coming around.

Well then it happened. SHRDLU suckered OSTRICH with a poisoned pawn. It was amazing. Several moves later OSTRICH had its only developed piece, the Queen, sitting on QN7 and SHRDLU had four pieces coming in on its opponent's King. Well as luck would have it, just at the moment SHRDLU had a mate in two, it noticed it was running short of time and dropped its search depth to two ply.

Newborn was furiously checking his listings and querying his personal on site Nova C.E. about the hardware.

SHRDLU made safe checking moves and picked up some material. "Why doesn't this lousy program get it over with?" said Newborn, coming full circle. Well SHRDLU administered the coup de grace on the 40th move (it was 40 moves in two hours). SHRDLU found a pretty mate as soon as it thought it had time to look.

Round 2

Only the devil could have invented the Swiss system. Paired against CHESS 4.4.

Slate had watched SHRDLU and was impressed. SHRDLU was playing nice chess for a mini. Slate is a gentleman and throughout the game we had pleasant conversation. SHRDLU searched 1200 to 5000 nodes during its move. It kept very accurate time control by having a separate interrupt key to signal the clock change. CHESS 4.4 on the CDC CYBER 175 searched more nodes per second than SHRDLU per move. Typical trees were 500K nodes and up.

SHRDLU held the initiative throughout the game. It made several deep tactical errors and CHESS 4.4 prevailed by brute force. But even in defeat, SHRDLU was threatening mate in three.

A note of interest here: During the chess programming panel discussion, Joel Moses of symbolic algebraic manipulation fame and Richard Greenblatt's boss, announced that Greenblatt had a hardware TTL chess machine under construction. 500K nodes per second!!! A full eight ply per second—and it only cost $10K.

Slate (Mr. Nodes-per-second) just held his head, quietly, in disbelief. And Levy, after a slight pause, asked, "Would Mr. Greenblatt care to increase my wager?" A man with real guts.

Simultaneous display by Levy against all the programs

Levy was in bad shape. He looked ill and complained of the jet lag. I have never seen him so out of sorts, and his play showed it. He actually permitted two draws.

SHRDLU held its own until it got into time trouble. Then it politely sped up, searched very shallow, and blew the game. By now it had established itself as a program to be reckoned with. Slate's favorable evaluation helped.

Round 3

E.S. vs. CHUTE 1.2. SHRDLU, the clearly superior program decimated CHUTE.

Martha managed the program while I went to a debate on SIL's (System Implementation Languages.) Newspaper people photographed her from every angle (the only girl). Neither she nor the monitor for CHUTE knew how to play chess. Fortunately both programs accepted algebraic notation.

Incidentally, the tournament set-up was the best I have ever seen. There were six large magnetic display boards with a side display pad for previous moves. Each table was equipped with a regular tourney set and a giant set with pawns 6" high. It was a great set up for the spectators and Richard Harbeck and his associates received well deserved congratulations.

Round 4

Once again that old Swiss system got us. (It isn't great but it is the fairest.) We were paired against Tony Marsland's WITA. WITA had only one win. If we had been paired against anyone with two wins then second place could have been ours on the break points.

By move 9 SHRDLU had WITA's King in the middle of the board. (A nice little sacrifice got it there.) Then SHRDLU did an amazing thing. It hardly ever searched more than four ply; but there it was progressively deepening what it thought was a good line. And it was! Announced mate in three. The fans went wild. Levy said "I'm sure E.S. will find this line. It has played surprisingly well in this tournament."

It was the shortest mate in tournament computer chess.

SHRDLU tied for second. The best mini-computer chess program yet. At the awards presentation, Jean Sammet handed me the first place trophy by mistake. Ben Mittman (of Northwestern) commented to Martha that SHRDLU deserved that prize.

Garth received the third place trophy based on the tie-breaking points. We had a gay old time congratulating him by phone. He modestly explained that he wasn't sure how good SHRDLU was because it always beat him!

Sincerely,

Richard J. Cichelli

References

A great deal of material in this book came from personal communications and the SIGART newsletters. A more formal list of references can be found in the *Proceedings of the First Computer Chess Conference* published by the Atlas Computer Laboratory, Science Research Council, Chilton, Oxfordshire.

Index

ACE computer 16, 29
ACM tournaments 41–48, 52, 54, 64, 65, 107
AI *see* Artificial intelligence
Alexander, C. H. O'D. 14
Algorithm 9
Alpha-beta 98
Artificial intelligence 23
Atkin, Larry 41–43, 48, 60, 64
Atkin, Ron 52, 80, 91, 92
ATLAS computer 26, 49–53, 80, 110

Babbage, Charles 12–13
Barricelli, Nils 49–50, 67
Berliner, Hans 45, 63–64, 76, 80–81
Bernstein, Alex 33–36
Birmingham, John 54, 76, 81, 101
Bletchley 13–17
Bobrow, Dan 41
Botvinnik, Mikhail 45, 91
Bowden, Lord 8, 16–17, 29, 35

Caswell, Thomas 72–75
Cathode ray tube *see* CRT
CHAOS 60–62
Checkers 28–29, 40, 93, 98
CHESS 3.0~4.4 41–44, 48, 55, 60–64, 76, 80–81, 102, 109
Chopper 99–100
Cichelli, Richard 103, 107–110
COKO 46–47, 101
Cooper, Dennis 47, 49
Courtois, Garth 108–110
CRT 15–16, 26–27

Dead position 18, 30, 39
de Groot, Adrian 89
Donskoy, Mikhail 63, 76
Draughts *see* Checkers
Dreyfus, Hubert 36–38

Eastlake, Donald 38–40
ELIZA 40–41
ENIAC computer 16, 31
ETAOIN SHRDLU 108–110
Euwe, Max 89–90

Feedover 100–101
Fine, Reuben 49
Fischer, Bobby 42, 45, 54

GENIE 46–47
Gillogly, James 42–43
Glennie, Alick 17–21
Golombek, Harry 14–15
Good, Jack 14, 44–45, 51
Greenblatt, Richard 38–41, 109

Hartston, Bill 79, 92–93
Horizon effect 29
Huberman, Barbara 36, 68–72

IFIPS 51

Jones, R. V. 14, 86

113